Lessons from God's Creation

Wisdom in Nature's Design

Rodney L. Rice

BLACKBERRY
BOOKS

Contents

Foreword

There was a time when I was far from what I am today. I was a rebellious kid, lost and without direction. But everything changed when I met the Lord. His love transformed me in ways I could never have imagined, and that transformation set me on a path to becoming a preacher.

Now, after fifty years of marriage, with a daughter married to a preacher, and a wonderful son, I look back and see how God has shaped my life and how His hand has been present every step of the way. In God's wonderful world, what can we learn from nature?

I share the lessons I've learned from my personal journey and the wisdom God has woven into creation. Nature is one of God's greatest teachers, filled with parables reflecting His love, purpose, and desire for us to walk closely with Him.

Throughout this book, you'll find stories drawn from the natural world, each offering insights into how we can grow spiritually and live out God's plan. Like the oak tree, steadfast and rooted, or the salmon fighting upstream against all odds, nature reflects our struggles, growth, and perseverance.

In these quiet moments of observing the world around us, we often hear God's voice the loudest. This book is not just a reflection on nature—it's a reflection on God's love for us, His creation. I hope that through these pages, you, too, will find inspiration to deepen your relationship with Him, trust in His guidance, and find joy in fulfilling His purpose for you. Let me know if this captures your thoughts or if you'd like further adjustments!

This book is a collection of reflections and a deeply personal exploration of the connection between nature and faith. Each chapter reminds us that, like the oak tree standing firm or the butterfly emerging from its cocoon, God has placed signs of His presence all around us. The author's gift lies in revealing these connections—helping us see that every leaf, every animal, and every drop of water points us back to the Creator.

As you read through the pages, you will be guided by parables illuminating timeless spiritual truths. These stories, drawn from nature, are windows into understanding God's purpose for our lives. You will be reminded that, much like the elements of creation fulfilling their role.

We, too, are called to live in alignment with God's will. As the author powerfully explains, only in fulfilling our purpose can we find true peace and happiness. This book is a call to slow down, appreciate the natural world with new eyes, and deepen your relationship with God.

Through the simple yet profound messages written into the fabric of creation. As you walk through each chapter, may you be encouraged to draw closer to God, trusting in His wisdom and care as reflected in His wonderful world. Let me know if you'd like to add or change anything!

Introduction

There was a mighty tree that grew by the riverbank. Its roots run deep, drinking from the calm waters, and its branches stretched high into the sky. It increased yearly, bearing fruit in season and offering shelter to birds and animals. How can individuals practically root themselves in God's Word to withstand life's trials, as the tree by the river does?

One year, a great drought came upon the land. The earth cracked, and many plants withered away. Yet, the tree by the river remained green, its leaves unfurling and its fruit abundant. Travelers passing by marveled at its strength.

When asked how it survived, the tree said, "The river roots me. Though the drought came, the river still flowed beneath the surface, nourishing me. My strength is not from the world above but from the waters below." Growth and resilience; while other trees dried up and fell, this tree stood tall and full of life.

What are some specific ways to slow down and connect with the natural world to discover its eternal truths? In learning

God's attributes through nature, what actions can people take to expand their spiritual knowledge and connection?

Psalm 1:3 NKJV

> *He shall be like a tree planted by the rivers of water, that brings forth its fruit in its season, whose leaf also shall not wither; And whatever he does shall prosper.*

In the same way, those who are rooted in God's word will find nourishment, even in times of distress, for their strength comes not from the passing things of the world but from the living water of the Spirit.

> In a world filled with chaos and agitation exists a silent masterpiece, a grand work of genius composed by the hands of an invisible sculptor. With its infinite beauty and complex design, nature is evidence of a higher power.
>
> Previous attempts to understand God in nature have yielded exciting results. In 1982, Biologist Arthur Jones reasoned that nature "will show plan and purpose" based on what Scripture reveals about God's sovereignty, wisdom, faithfulness, and promises.[1]

During our journey, we will be led to the proof; let us slow down our speedy existence to realize the eternal truths nature so kindly presents us. Let us engage in the stroke of genius of creation. Join me as we resolve the structures of this divine creation.

---

1. Jones Tony, 30 September 2024 *Wikipedia*, the free encyclopedia.

Ecclesiastes 3:11

> *He has made everything beautiful in its time. Also, He has put*
> *eternity in their hearts, except that no one can find out the*
> *work God does from beginning to end.*

1 John 1:3

> *That which we have seen and heard we declare to you, that you*
> *also may have fellowship with us; and truly our fellowship is*
> *with the Father and His Son Jesus Christ.*

As dark clouds gather in the distance, the oak tree stands
steady. Its thick and early branches spread upward, silently
preparing for the storm. Lower in the ground, the tree roots are
observed to be greater, locating strength hidden to the eye. The
animals around it know that change is coming. Some rush
through to safety, while others stop, detecting what the winds
will carry.

Our lives are like nature, filled with seasons with storms
and calmness. The struggling times will come. It is not whether
storms will come but how prepared we are when they do. This
book studies the knowledge that can be learned through nature,
where each living thing demonstrates challenges that can teach
us about God's attributes in the Bible.

> The scientific investigation of creation biology research ques-
> tions has already revealed displays of God's omniscience,
> omnipotence, and foreknowledge. By studying which plants
> constitute a single "kind," Todd Wood and David Cavanaugh

found that God hard-wired into the genetics of these species the information to deal with post-flood environments.[2]

Jeremiah 17:8

For he shall be like a tree planted by the waters, which spreads out its roots by the river and will not fear when heat comes; But its leaf will be green and will not be anxious in the year of drought, nor will cease from yielding fruit.

When I was a young father, my family and I used to lie on a quilt in the yard, staring up at the sky, searching for the Zodiac signs hidden among the stars. My wife would point out the different constellations she knew, and I would squint, hoping to see them. Yet, no matter how hard I tried, I could only ever find the Big and Little Dipper.

The sky's vastness and the stars' beauty are hard to comprehend, yet they are noticeable. Though I could not understand all the constellations, the ones I could see were enough to inspire astonishment. In the same way, life can feel like that: looking for answers or meaning.

Just as the stars follow their patterns in the heavens, nature reflects a pattern and commitment we often overlook. Animals and plants prepare for the coming storms; they do not fear or wonder why the storm is coming; they trust the path, instinctively knowing they can survive it.

In the same way, God calls us to spiritual commitment. We may not see the entire image of His plan, just as I could not see all the constellations, but we can trust that the parts we reach, the signs of His hand in the world, are enough to direct us.

God is transcendent; therefore, He cannot be adequately

---

2. Wood, T. C. (n.d.).

illustrated by anything that belongs to creation. A simple example suffices to make this point. Since God, in His nature, is eternal and uncreated, nothing in His created universe qualifies to illustrate both characteristics.

> Yet, because the creation of God bears undeniable evidence of its Author, there are things in nature that may reflect—even though in a very pale way—some of the characteristics of the nature of God. What follows are two analogies from physics that can serve as illustrations for aspects of the Divinity, starting from the premise that what we can know of God is founded on what He has revealed to us through the Holy Scriptures. Therefore, our endeavor to grasp a vision of God through His creation will be directed and restricted to what the Scriptures reveal about the nature of God, for what goes beyond that is pure speculation.[3]

We can avoid developing a thankful heart. We might get submerged in daily encounters, like sickness, or overloaded with financial circumstances. One way to grow appreciation is to search the history of God's blessings, starting right when He created the world with its creatures and the people He made in His image.

Daniel 12:3

> *Those who are wise will shine like the brightness of the heavens, and those who lead many to righteousness, like the stars forever and ever.*

I was raised in a city with many lights in California and had

---

3. Augustine of Hippo. (n.d.). (5. V. *Zondervan Pictorial Encyclopedia of the Bible*).

never seen so many stars appear until my family and I drove into the state of Arkansas; that's where I met my wife. Guess what happens when you marry a girl with beautiful memories of being in nature as part of her life. You guessed it, I learned to enjoy nature in a new way.

My wife and I have enjoyed many vacations where we went tent camping, not to be confused with the luxury of being in an RV. There is a difference. Having your family in a tent is an experience. As a family, we have enjoyed God's creation; there was always something that got our attention. Ants, hornets, and raccoons would get into our groceries. Gladly, we were never visited by any bears. One thing that we were constantly entertained by was squirrels.

Romans 1:20

For since the world's creation, His invisible attributes are seen, being understood by the things that are made, even His eternal power and Godhead, so that they are without excuse.

God made all things; He is excellent, good, perfect, and outstanding. He reaches out to us. My prayers go out to those who cannot see all the blessings our Great God has designed for us to enjoy.

As Christians, we must reach out to others. God has stated in His Word that those born again should share that astonishing experience with as many people as possible. In this age when multitudes are given to greed and pride and sex and self-will, the church is quiet about God's wrath. Instead, many church leaders ramble on and on about God's kindness—saying nothing about His judgment. How often, in the past year or two, have you heard a sermon about the wrath of God?[4]

---

4. John Piper. *The Pleasure of God.*

Those who do not know about God's wrath face a terrible situation. Consider someone in a house that is on fire with someone in it that is asleep. Would we do everything we could to wake them up before they became a victim? That's how we should look at those lost and without hope.

I'm afraid there is no fear of God. Many think we have only one life to live, so we must live it up with everything this world offers. That is not true; eternal life is yet to come, and all that we do or do not do will reflect where that will be spent. We need to spread the truth worldwide, which starts in our neighborhood. Just like the person in the burning house, there is not much time left to get them out of danger.

John 13: 34–35

A new commandment I give to you, that you love one another; as I have loved you, you also love one another. By this, all will know that you are My disciples if you have love for one another.

Psalm 63:6–8

When I remember you on my bed, I meditate on You in the night watches. Because You have been my help, I will rejoice in the shadow of Your wings. My soul follows close behind You; Your right hand upholds me.

A witness to others about Christ is someone who shows their faith in Jesus Christ through their words, actions, and attitude. Christians are witnesses to Jesus Christ because they know Him, experience His love, and testify to what He is up to in their lives and the church.

1 Peter 3:15

> *But sanctify the Lord God in your hearts, and always be ready*
> *to give a defense to everyone who asks you a reason for the hope*
> *that is in you, with meekness and fear;*

To understand the values, we can learn by slowing down and looking at what God has created. We will never doubt what He can do to ensure our lives are in order. We see how God's creation performs steadily according to their design.

Matthew 22:37–40

> *Jesus said to him, 'You shall love the Lord your God with all*
> *your heart, with all your soul, and with all your mind.' This is*
> *the first and great commandment. And the second is like it:*
> *'You shall love your neighbor as yourself.' On these two*
> *commandments hang all the Law and the Prophets.*

Chapter 1

The Blessing of the Sunlight

A town is nestled in a valley that depends on the sun for all it has. The villagers rise with the dawn each morning, working the fields and tending their homes under its light. Though they see the sun each day, few truly understand its significance. Some take its warmth for granted, and some complain when it shines too brightly or hides behind clouds.

One day, the sun disappeared from the sky. The villagers awoke to darkness, and the crops began to wither. Fear spread quickly through the village. They sought out the elders, asking how they could bring back the sun. The elders said wisely, "The sun has always been there, even when we forget its importance. We have not honored its gift."

Together, the village gathered to reflect on the sun's blessings: the food they ate, the warmth that protected them, and the light that guided them. With humble hearts, they turned their faces to the sky, no longer taking its presence for granted.

In time, the sun returned, shining even brighter than before. The villagers rejoiced, now understanding that though they couldn't control the sun, they could choose to appreciate it. They lived with tremendous gratitude, never forgetting the light sustaining their lives.

In the same way, God's presence in our lives is constant, whether we notice it or not. Like the sun, His grace sustains us, and when we turn our hearts to Him, we are reminded of the light and warmth He provides.

Just as the sun is steady and dependable, so is God's presence. When clouds cover the sky, the sun remains, shining behind them. We might not always see it, but we trust its unwavering presence. Likewise, in moments of doubt or hardship, when life seems clouded by trials, God's light remains constant, sustaining us through the darkest times.

Psalm 84:11

> For the Lord God is a sun and shield; The Lord will give grace and glory; No good thing will He withhold from those who walk uprightly.

Like the sun, God's light provides clarity, strength, and guidance to His people, offering protection and grace along the way. Jesus is the sun in the sense of spiritual life. Without Him, we remain in darkness.

But—the sun's light drives away darkness daily, reminding us of the victory of light over darkness. Similarly, Jesus dispels the darkness of sin and evil, bringing hope and redemption to the world.

Jesus is like the sun, bringing life, guidance, and warmth to a world otherwise lost in darkness. By understanding the significance of the sun, we can better grasp the powerful truth of Jesus as the light of the world, shining on all who follow Him.

A quote by the poet Walt Whitman. "Keep your face always towards the sunshine, and shadows will fall behind you."

This simple truth had never occurred to me in any cognizant way. When you face the sun, you never see the darkness behind you. How many times have I faced the sun without noticing that?[1]

As nature responds to the sun's presence, God has called us to respond to His light. The sun's power is life-giving—trees grow, flowers bloom, and animals awaken because of its energy. Similarly, our spiritual lives flourish when we relish in the light of God's Word, allowing His truth to guide and sustain us. Without the sun, life on earth would wither and fade; without God, our souls would be dark and lifeless.

1 John 1:5

This is the message which we have heard from Him and declare to you, that God is light and in Him is no darkness at all.

Just as the sun lights the way for us, revealing our surroundings and guiding us, Jesus informs our path in life. His teachings help us see clearly what is right and wrong and lead us to righteousness.

We know God is love, and His word clarifies this throughout the Bible. His Word tells us that we are saved by grace through faith. That means this salvation is available to anyone as a gift from God.

So, what are we waiting for? Many have not accepted God's invitation. It may be that we, as Christians, have failed to

---

1. M. B. Whitman, "Keep Your Face Always Towards the Sunshine, and the Shadows Will Fall Behind You," March 5, 2019, https://quoteinvestigator. com/2019/03/05/sunshine/

spread the Word. They may not know how accurate this gift of God is or about that place called hell.

It is a very alarming situation in our world; so many live as if this world is all that there is. We have not accepted what God has shown us in His Word, written by people there with Jesus —telling us to spread the Word before it is too late.

Feeling Jesus's love encourages us to share that love with others. We know Jesus has called us all to spread the gospel, yet evangelizing can be difficult. Nonetheless, through God's motivation, we can share our faith in ways that influence people to pay attention and become interested in hearing more. Joy is easy to share; people already see it in your actions.

Just as the sun is steady and dependable, so is God's presence. When clouds cover the sky, the sun remains, shining behind them. We might not always see it, but we trust its unwavering presence. Likewise, in moments of doubt or difficulty, life seems clouded by trials.

Even when clouds hide the sun, it stays present and alive, providing light and warmth. Likewise, a Christian's impact may not always be seen directly, but through constant faith and prayer, they continue to affect the world, knowing that God is always at work, even in invisible ways. The sun can illustrate a Christian's role in the world—bringing light, warmth, and growth.[2]

As Christians, we should resemble the sun in usefulness. What a dark world this would be if the natural sun ceased shining. What would the world be without Christianity? As the sun rises above the clouds and darkness, the believer rises above the fluctuations and hardships of life; they dismiss the mists and darkness of prejudgment and prove that Christianity does not

2. C. S. Lewis, (1952, N/A N/A). *Mere Christianity*. N/A: HarperCollins. Retrieved from *Mere Christianity*.

tend to inaccuracy and is not a system of misery. Like the sun, Christianity spreads the most valuable and beautiful influences worldwide.

The sun is the great spirit of the world, in the light of which all things are made to rejoice. So, the Christian's life and the compassionate efforts of the Church connect with God's Divine power, who can do whatever He wants. Each believer needs never to forget that everything that was created was created by God.

Numbers 6:24–26

The Lord bless you and keep you; The Lord make His face shine upon you And be gracious to you; The Lord lift up His countenance upon you, And give you peace.

Matthew 5:16

Let your light so shine before men, that they may see your good works, and glorify your Father which is in heaven.

Sharing how Jesus has changed your life. How you have received such great hope. This is what Christians do! The devastating state of the lost should be urgent to your heart. Telling others about the love God has shown us through Jesus is like spreading the idea that you have found the cure for some terrible disease.

You would not hesitate to inform people about the cure, knowing it would save their lives. Isn't knowing the cure for everlasting death in the fire of hell more critical? We know the cure—it's salvation through our savior, Jesus Christ.

Let's go out and share the message of God's love, the creator of all things, including the sacrifice of His only begotten Son to pay the price for our sins. Nothing is more significant than

God's love; we should tell the world about it. Just as Jesus reached out to the lost, we must continue to do the same.

Matthew 9:37

Then He said to His disciples, "The harvest truly is plentiful, but the laborers are few."

Perhaps many of us are too involved in our daily lives to reach out to lost people. Sometimes, we forget that Jesus could come anytime, and many people are not ready. First, we need to be prepared, and then we need to reach out to family and friends.

As opportunity leads you to others, we must witness to them. Tell as many as we can that they need to be ready. Let's reveal our light so that those in darkness see Christ through us. Being excited about your salvation will light up the room and show others that there is still joy in the world.

There are so many traps throughout this world that many people are in distress because they do not know how to escape their mess. Without the leadership of Christ, the devil will destroy them with his sinful devices. The devil is out to destroy God's creation of humanity, and he will do whatever he can to accomplish it.

Modern science tells us how special our sun is and how it relates to our planet. Without going into too much of that science, the Earth's distance from the sun is perfect. Scientists call that distance the Goldilocks zone because it is "just right." The sun not only gives us light, but it also gives us the energy we all use to go about our daily lives.

As science class taught us, plants produce energy from the sun's light. Animals eat those plants and store energy in their bodies. We either eat the plants directly or eat the meat of the animals for energy. Either way, our life-giving energy comes from the sun.

Life and our decisions often bring clouds that block our view of Jesus. When that happens, we sometimes notice troubles we ignore when we enjoy His light. To stay in the sunlight of Christ, the Bible calls us to stay in God's word, stay close to other believers, stay in prayer, and live with gratitude. When we do such things, the light of Christ will continue to bring us warmth, life, and joy.[3]

The Psalmist has determined that God will become our sunshine, sheltering those who accept the gift of salvation through His Son, the Lord Jesus Christ. Through our relationship with Him, we will have access to His blessings. The grace God has made possible through Christ is a gift we do not deserve. This should allow us to acknowledge the greatness of His love.

God wraps His love around us in a way that will bless our lives, allowing us to live in righteousness that appears within our Lord Jesus Christ. Through the guidance of our Lord, we are never alone in facing the world's difficulties. When you think about how blessed the child of God is to have His presence in every aspect of our lives, the journey does not seem that difficult, knowing that you are being led by a guide who knows the way.

Without the light from the sun, life would not survive. The sun is needed to bring life to God's nature. As His children, we need the light from Christ, the love that lights up a dark world. At one time, I lived in this dark world full of sin, and then Jesus came and lit up my entire world.

I knew several people I hung out with who never saw the

---

3. Reyna L. Aburto, LDS Living. A Division of Deseret Book Company, 2024.

age of twenty because of how we lived. God has shown me a lot of mercy and given me a life I do not deserve. Even when I let Him down, He still showed me love and led me away from the mess that I got into. The things offered by the world do not seem so interesting once you have experienced the difficulties that go with them. Each time I got caught up in the tricks of the devil, destruction followed. The bad part of all this is that I knew that this was not a place that I should be.

This is why the Bible teaches us to fight to stay focused. An enemy is working around the clock to destroy us, so doesn't it make sense that we must try to stay alert and prepared for the Devil's invasion? The plan has already been written, and it's all in the Bible.

Knowing that the enemy is trying to destroy us, we should never start a day or finish one without prayer and the reading of God's Word. We can't just sit back and pretend that there is no evil power through the devil who wants us to fail.

Chapter 2

Finding Wisdom in the Stars

A young shepherd once wandered the vast plains, guiding his flock under the wide, open sky. Every night, he would look up at the stars, marveling at their brilliance but never knowing their purpose. One evening, he lost his way. The familiar paths were hidden in the darkness, and fear gripped his heart.

Desperate and unsure, he gazed upward again, searching the heavens for guidance. He noticed that certain stars never changed their place in the sky. They formed patterns like a map etched in light. Trusting in their steady presence, he followed them, and by dawn, he found his way home.

As he sat by the fire, the shepherd realized the stars had always been fixed and constant, pointing toward safety. He thought to himself, If the stars, so distant and silent, can guide me in my hour of need, how much more does God, who placed them there, desire to guide my heart?

From that day, every time the shepherd looked to the stars, it reminded him of God's unfailing presence, drawing the shepherd closer to His will. Just as the stars guide travelers through the night, God's presence guides us through the darkness of life.

When we look at the heavens, God's children are reminded of His vastness and His care for even the smallest details of creation. The stars call us to lift our eyes toward God and find comfort in His eternal persistence.

Consider the stars. Do you know the number of stars out there? There are too many for me to count. Looking up at the stars reminds us of God's greatness and power.

There would be so much darkness at night without the stars, just as there would be in our world without the children of God

Colossians 2: 9–10

For in Him dwells all the fullness of the Godhead bodily, and you are complete in Him, who is the head of all principality and power,

God has promised never to leave us, never to forsake us. Even if it feels like He has withdrawn from us, He is there, strong, mighty, tender, and beautiful. Like the obstruction of city lights hiding the power of the stars, clutter in our lives lessens the glory of the Lord, causing us to feel alone in our pain.

Psalm 147:4–5

He counts the number of the stars; He calls them all by name. Great is our Lord, and mighty in power; His understanding is infinite.

I find it interesting that the stars stay where God put them. That is how travelers in ancient times were able to navigate through the night.

Zephaniah 3:17

The Lord your God in your midst, The Mighty One, will save;
He will rejoice over you with gladness; he will quiet you with
His love; he will rejoice over you with singing.

Constant, symbolizing God's faithfulness. This can be a comforting reminder of His enduring presence, even when life seems uncertain. The stars have been the navigation system for centuries, guiding sailors and travelers. We, too, are guided by His light in the darkness of this world that overshadows our lives.

Though stars are far away and seem small from Earth, their size and power are massive. Though sometimes subtle, God's presence in our lives is far greater and more powerful than we often perceive.

Centuries ago, God provided direction in our lives. The vast number of stars can remind us of the infinite nature of God's promises, power, and love. Even when the stars seem distant or hard to see, in the same manner as God is at times, their light is always there.

Additionally, you could explore how stars, though far away, play an essential role in the universe, just as God's influence shapes our lives from a perspective greater than we can often see or understand. This approach ties together the theme of stars and their reflection of God's greatness and purpose.

Psalm 19:1

The heavens declare the glory of God, And the firmament
shows His hand.

When we watch the night sky and observe the twinkling stars, we should be thoughtful of God's unlimited power and creativity. Just as the stars light up the darkness of the night, so too can we be a guiding light of God's light in a world hidden in spiritual darkness. Like the stars, our lives can point others toward our Heavenly Father's glory and devotion. Furthermore, the stars are a constant and steady testimony to God's reliability and faithfulness.

Isaiah 60:1

For your light has come! And the glory of the Lord is risen upon you.

Isaiah 40:26

Lift your eyes on high, and see who has created these things, who brings out their host by number; He calls them all by name, By the greatness of His might and the strength of His power; Not one is missing.

The journey of a star mirrors our spiritual journey. We are "born" in faith, nurtured by the Word of God. Our faith shines brightly as we grow, just as a star does in its prime. Yet, like the stars, we, too, face challenges and moments where our light seems dim. But even in these moments, the Bible teaches each believer that there is a renewal.

2 Corinthians 4:16

Therefore, we do not lose heart. Even though our outward man is perishing, the inward man is renewed daily.

As stars go through cycles, so do we in our walk with God. Faith requires constant renewal, just like stars fueled by the fusion of elements in their core. The power of God works within us, keeping our inner flame burning, even in seasons of difficulty. We look up at the stars; it's hard not to feel a sense of awe. For centuries, people have lifted their eyes to the heavens, finding inspiration in the beauty and mystery of the stars.

The massiveness of space can make us feel small, but it also calls us to worship something far more significant than ourselves. Stars, in their brilliance, point us toward the Creator. They remind us that we are part of something much bigger, something divine.

Like the stars, each of God's children reflects the light of God's glory. When we worship, we are like stars shining in the night, declaring the goodness and majesty of the One who made us. It shifts our focus away from the troubles of this world and lifts our eyes to the eternal. Stars stand as silent witnesses to the greatness of God, urging us to join creation in praise. As we watch upon the celestial heavens, the magnificent handiwork of our Creator.

The stars, placed in their courses by the divine wisdom of God, speak to us of His power, glory, and faithfulness. The actual size of the universe demonstrates, as does God's intensity.

He looked up at the stars and realized that God named each one. I could not even count how many there are; seeing how they can lead people to their destination is beyond my understanding, as are the celestial bodies. It shows us how great our God is and how we should know that we should not worry about anything if He can do this. God has control of all His creation.

> The stars were put there to tell a story, which was, in fact, the most incredible story that would ever be told. It was an epic indeed. And since the fall of man in the garden, man has been born with a craving ... a desire to know that story. Indeed, this is also a part of God's grace. He is always reaching out to

men. His love towards man has never changed; his desire that none perish has never changed.

There is a Christ-shaped void and therefore only Christ can fill it. That's why Satan has so many things to offer to man to fill the void, but only Christ will truly fill it completely. Satan has done his best to corrupt that story in fact it has been hidden from us because he is the villain in the story who hates us and wants to destroy us. Wants to limit the role that we will accept in that story.[1]

The stars shine brightly in the darkness, illuminating the night with their majesty. In the same way, as followers of Christ, Christians live to be the light of the world, shining forth the love and truth of God in a world filled with darkness and despair.

One of the best ways to share your faith is to live a godly life. Christians often look to show those close to them that they care by spending time with them, helping them meet their needs, and offering to listen when they have difficulties.

You might not be able to resolve all their questions, but they can't reject the reality of Christ's actions in your life. Another essential part of sharing your faith is to pray for those you interact with. If you can't think of anyone who isn't a Christian, pray for God to place someone in your life who needs Him.

2 Corinthians 4:6

For it is the God who commanded the light to shine out of darkness, who has shone in our hearts to give the light of the knowledge of the glory of God in the face of Jesus Christ.

1. McLaughlin, R. (2024, October Friday). *The Gospel of Jesus Christ is written in the Stars.* Retrieved from letters@gbible.org:
   https://gbible.org/tree-of-life-post/gosple-jesus-christ-written-stars/

As Christians, we should reflect God's love in our hearts. We want others to be attracted to the light that shines from Christ's love and wonder where all that kindness comes from.

Everyone should know that humanity's journey starts with sin. We all have sinned and fallen short of God's glory. It does not have to remain that way; the gift of salvation will give us a new journey with greater hope through Christ.

Romans 3:23

For all have sinned and fall short of the glory of God.

With this understanding, all humanity must seek salvation for their souls. The big question is, do you know someone who has not accepted the Lord to reach for eternal life in heaven? Then, let your light shine so bright that those people will see Christ. There is no more significant victory than leading someone to the Lord.

Yet, this will not happen if we talk about witnessing. Children of God should leave their comfort zones and reach out to the lost like the stars. Let your lights shine. Even in the world of darkness, our light should show through. As the stars give us light at night, we should put forth a light of Christ for the lost.

Your life's change should open many doors for you to tell others what caused that change and how great it has been. Since you have accepted Christ as your savior, life has a more perfect meaning, and you want everyone to know.

Let your light shine with the love that came into us by the grace of God. Through this grace, He has cleaned us from our sins, and now His love has filled our hearts. With that kind of love, we will attract others who want to know how we can remain happy in the situation that is taking place at that time.

Psalm 145:3–5

Great is the LORD, and greatly to be praised, And His great-ness is unsearchable.

One generation shall praise Your works to another And shall declare Your mighty acts.

I will meditate on the glorious splendor of Your majesty And on Your wondrous works.

Chapter 3

Can You See the Wind?

There were once two winds, the gentle wind and the fierce wind, who often argued over which had more power. The main intense wind boasted its ability to uproot trees and tear down houses, while the gentle wind was quiet. One day, they encountered a traveler walking along the road, wrapped in a cloak.

The fierce wind said, "Watch me. I will force him to remove his cloak." It blew with all its might, thrashing the trees and shaking the earth. But the more complex the wind blew, the tighter the traveler held onto his cloak, wrapping it closer to his body.

Then, the gentle wind took its turn. It began to blow softly, just enough to ruffle the leaves and cool the air. Slowly, the traveler loosened his grip on his cloak until he finally removed it, laying it aside to enjoy the breeze.

The fierce wind, humbled, learned that true strength lies not in force but in subtlety and patience. As the wind is free to blow at any time, so the Spirit of God is a free agent in rebirth; He works how, where, and when He pleases. He acts freely in the first operation of His grace on the heart and in all after influences of it, as well as in the donation of His gifts to men, for different purposes.

1 Corinthians 12:11

But the same Spirit works all these things, distributing to each one individually as He wills.

In the book of John, our Lord Jesus Christ speaks of the wind in a discourse with Nicodemus, relating the work of the Spirit to the wind, blowing where it wishes, unseen yet intensely felt by its effects (John 3:8). Here, the wind indicates the peculiar, outstanding work of the Holy Spirit in repairing hearts and bringing about spiritual rebirth. The scriptures deliver the work of the Holy Spirit, the accomplishment of human life, and the authority of our Almighty Creator.

John 3:8

The wind blows where it wishes, and you hear it but cannot tell where it comes from and where it goes. So is everyone who is born of the Spirit.

The wind moves unseen, much like the hand of God, guiding all things in silence.

We do not see where it begins or ends, yet its presence is inevitable. In the same way, God's effect on our lives often goes ignored, but His hand is always at work, influencing the road of our journey.

As the wind stimulates the trees, rustling their leaves with a gentle force, so does God stir the hearts of His people. His presence may come softly, like a breeze, or fiercely like a storm, but it always reaches us. God's progress in our lives is sometimes quiet, yet it carries the strength to change everything.

The Spirit of God works in ways we may not comprehend, but we know His presence guides us. When we cannot see God, His breath on earth reminds us of His continual care. Just as the wind brings life to a barren landscape, so does God breathe life into our souls, renewing us and giving us strength for the journey ahead. We can feel His power in every breeze and see God's intimate connection with His creation.

We do not see where it begins or ends, yet its presence is undeniable. In the same way, God's influence in our lives often goes unnoticed, but His hand is always at work. We must become aware of God's presence, remembering He is there to help and guide us through every aspect of life.

God is only waiting for us to call Him; the scriptures teach us to ask, and then we will receive. We like to try to handle things for ourselves; we must realize there is an enemy with great power, which we cannot fight against through our power.

Faith, like the wind, is abstract, metaphysical, and intangible. You cannot see the wind; you cannot see faith. So, how does one know that such a thing as "wind" exists? Because one sees the evidence of the wind. Leaves rustling, papers blowing, clouds moving–these all tell us that air is moving, and we call it "wind." When we hear the air whistling or rushing past our ears, leaves rustling, or papers blowing, we attribute it to air movement. When we feel air glide over our skin or blow dust in our eyes, we know there is a wind at that moment–and so it is with faith and work. Good deeds tell us that a person has faith that the promises of God are sure and that His rewards are more significant than the temptations of sin. Evil deeds show an absence of such faith.[1]

---

1. A.W, Tozer, "In The Pursuit of God," https://www.goodreads.com/work/ quotes/203894-the-pursuit-of-god

Jesus died on the cross and overcame the devil. He conquered death by rising on the third day so we could be presented as people without sin. He died, and His blood has cleansed everyone who has received the gift of salvation. We are children of God, and if there are situations that you cannot handle, call on God through prayer, and then you will use His great power.

The wind is often interpreted as a representation of change and direction. How the wind blows, and its force can be interpreted in numerous ways. Wind can be seen as a force of change that brings in new hopes and moves away from the old. It can also be seen as a leading force that directs us towards our goals.

Exodus 14:21–22

Then Moses stretched out his hand over the sea, and the LORD caused the sea to go back by a strong east wind all that night, and made the sea into dry land, and the waters were divided. So, the children of Israel went into the midst of the sea on the dry ground, and the waters were a wall to them on their right hand and their left.

In the book of Exodus, we are shown how God used the power of the wind to part the sea. This same power is with us through His Holy Spirit, assuring us of His ability to see us through life's difficulties.

When we face trials and temptations alone, there seems to be no hope of overcoming the situations. Instead, we should give it all to God, and just like the wind, He will blow it away. Even though we cannot see God or His Holy Spirit, our life experiences tend to change without knowing where the change came from.

That is an excellent example of the power of our God. If

He speaks it, then it is so. In the same way, His Holy Spirit can change our lives in various ways. When we think there is no hope, God intervenes through the power of the Holy Spirit.

Genesis 8:1

Then God remembered Noah, every living thing, and all the animals with him in the ark. And God made a wind to pass over the earth, and the waters subsided.

Just think how mighty the wind was drying away the flood that destroyed everything outside the ark. This same force is there for us, even when we put ourselves in circumstances that should have been prevented.

Like the wind, the Holy Spirit can remove objects that have brought us to a low state of mind and feelings of hopelessness. Putting God first will help you understand His will. Sometimes, you must stop and listen to what the Holy Spirit says.

Jesus explained the same power when He told Nicodemus that the new birth begins like a blowing wind. It is something you cannot see, but it can be felt. When we accept Jesus Christ as our savior, at that moment, it is like the wind blowing through us; the presence of our creator is there.

John 3:5–8

Jesus answered, Most assuredly, I say to you, unless one is born of water and the Spirit, he cannot enter the kingdom of God. That which is born of the flesh is flesh, and that which is born of the Spirit is spirit. Do not marvel that I said to you, 'You must be born again.' The wind blows where it wishes, and you hear it but cannot tell where it comes from and where it goes. So is everyone who is born of the Spirit.

Paul tells us how the flesh and the Spirit oppose each other, something every believer can connect with. This battle is part of our enduring battle against the world, the flesh, and the Devil as the Holy Spirit works to make us increasingly more like Jesus. Sometimes, we can grow weary and discouraged by this struggle and even doubt our salvation. That is why we need the Bible to enhance our journey through life. There will come situations that are beyond our understanding.

Walking by the Spirit is the path to defeating the desires of the flesh and living a holy life. What a great encouragement to know that we don't have to stay stuck in our sins in an endless fearful cycle of defeat after defeat with no way out!

Some specific examples help us better understand the struggle between the Spirit and the flesh. What we surrender to will decide the path that will become our journey and where it leads. Knowing the difference is an integral part of reaching the right goal. The Bible gives us the right path to follow. When we read and study God's Word, it will set us in the right place.

Galatians 5:19–26

> I say then: Walk in the Spirit, and you shall not fulfill the lust of the flesh. The flesh lusts against the Spirit, and the Spirit against the flesh; these are contrary to one another so that you do not do the things you wish. But if you are led by the Spirit, you are not under the law. Now the works of the flesh are evident, which uncleanness, are: adultery, fornication, lewdness, idolatry, sorcery, hatred, contentions, jealousies, outbursts of wrath, selfish ambitions, dissensions, heresies, envy, murders, drunkenness, revelries, and the like; of which I tell you beforehand, just as I also told you in time past, that those who practice such things will not inherit the kingdom of God. But the fruit of the Spirit is love, joy, peace, longsuffering, kindness, goodness, faithfulness, gentleness, and self-control. Against such, there is no law. And those who are Christ's have

crucified the flesh with its passions and desires. If we live in the Spirit, let us also walk in the Spirit."

You can only be fruitful once you pull out the weeds. I have an exciting weed in my front yard. It is fragile and grass-like, but it grows up next to a plant and is winding around it. What it is trying to do is encompass the plant. It is stealing the resources and trying to choke out the plant as it wraps itself around it. These two cannot co-exist. The weeds must be removed. It would be best if you crucified the flesh with its passions and desires. I must stop thinking that I am walking with God when I am allowing any of these sins to continue to be practiced in my life. Now, hear what I said. We are allowing these sins to remain in our lives. Paul said that we have the choice to crucify these desires and passions. Paul said that those who belong to Jesus have killed the flesh. The desires and the passions of the flesh are obvious. You know what your issues are. You know where you need to fight. You know what desires need to be crucified. You know you cannot keep living like this and remain in the kingdom of God. Today is the day to fight back. Do not put it off any longer. Today is the day to go into the garden of your heart and tear out the weeds that are growing in there. Your soul is far too valuable to let the weeds keep growing. (10)^2

2.　Georg D. Touy, *Crucify The Flesh.*

Chapter 4

The Great Oak Tree

An ancient oak tree stood revered in a grand forest for its strength and wisdom. This oak was home to a squirrel, who built her nest high among its sturdy branches. The oak and the squirrel shared a deep bond; the oak provided shelter and nourishment, while the squirrel, in turn, tended to the tree's lower branches, keeping them free of pests.

One day, a strong windstorm swept through the forest. The oak stood firm with its deep roots and robust trunk, but the squirrel's nest was in danger of being blown away. The squirrel was anxious and worried about her home.

As the storm raged, the oak gently told the squirrel, "Fear not, little one. Though the storm is fierce, I shall stand steadfast. Trust in my strength, and know that even if your nest is damaged, we will rebuild together."

After the storm, the squirrel found that her nest had indeed been affected, but the oak's strength had preserved her home. Together, they repaired the damage and strengthened their bond.

The oak then shared a lesson with the squirrel: "Just as the oak tree withstands the storms with its roots and trunk, so too must we find strength in our walk with the Lord. Trust and assistance enable us to weather any storm."

Above ground, the trees offer food, shelter, and shade and help clean the air. Below the ground, the roots search for the water supply that they need to survive—about 50 gallons a day is the average amount. The oak tree's strength and endurance are a sign for Christians to be strong in their faith. The oak tree's roots continue to grow deeper and more established, representing the never-ending thirst for spirituality.

The oak tree's canopy provides shelter and protection to those beneath it. The oak tree can represent the body of Christ, which offers food for the world and survives through challenges. The oak tree can symbolize hospitality, stability, strength, honor, eternity, and endurance. In the Bible, God repeatedly uses the image of His people being like trees. Oak trees are known for their strength and strong root systems, which continue to grow, reaching out for the nourishment needed to keep growing. When you see an oak tree, you only see half of it, for its giant root systems extend much further than the tree's expanse—much of why oak trees flourish is below the surface.

Their root system is ever expanding under the ground as they continually search for water and nutrients for more and more growth and health for the tree above. Oak trees can apparently drink up to 50 gallons a day of water. Also, trees firmly planted with strong root systems can withstand fierce storms and live for hundreds of years. God desires us to have a good foundation, and he is even more concerned with our root system than our visible outward growth. A good root system will naturally support a tree to mature and grow with flowers or fruit in time.

Sometimes we are in such a rush to get instant answers from God, but meanwhile, He is trying to help establish us first firmly in His love and truths.[1]

The old saying goes, "You are what you eat." If we feed only on what the world offers, we will become like the world. God will become farther away as if we never knew Him. Only through continual growth will Christians be able to experience the love of Christ attending to our difficulties. Praying to Him and reading the Bible is a must to grow spiritually.

I worked at a sawmill during the early years of my marriage. Although it was hard, I enjoyed it sometimes. While stacking lumber from the green chain, suddenly, there was a loud noise, and everything stopped; a horseshoe was in the middle of the log being cut. The sawyer could not see it, so the blade hit the horseshoe and tore the teeth off.

This is like the oak tree; something nailed to it does not stop it, and the tree will grow around it. Christians should never let the past destroy the future; instead, let it be a lesson to gain future gain in the Lord. Just as the oak tree continues to grow, those who walk with the Lord should do the same.

Psalm 1:1–3

Blessed is the man who walks not in the counsel of the ungodly, Nor stands in the path of sinners, nor sits in the seat of the scornful. But his delight is in the law of the LORD, And in His law, he meditates day and night. He shall be like a tree planted by the rivers of water, that brings forth its fruit in its season, whose leaf also shall not wither; And whatever he does shall prosper.

---

1. B.K.M. (Kenny) Gorrel, *The Hidden Places Where God Develops.*

The oak tree knows the importance of water, so its roots are always reaching out to find more as needed. Nobody must tell the tree it is time to start looking for more water; instinct speaks to nature, and they respond to it. Christians should respond to the Spirit of God who dwells within us. Pay attention and understand that it is time to start building on your relationship with Christ. Reaching out and seeking the water of life through His Word should come naturally.

John 7:37–38

> *On the last day, that great day of the feast, Jesus stood and cried out, saying, "If anyone thirsts, let him come to Me and drink. He who believes in Me, as the Scripture has said, out of his heart will flow rivers of living water."*

The living water is the Holy Spirit. Jesus offered everyone the belief that faith in Him leads us to salvation. The result of salvation would be the gift of the Holy Spirit. Related unto rivers of living water. The picture of the Spirit as "living water" leads us to the following conclusions. Just as water refreshes and revives a thirsty person, the Spirit gives life to the believer.

The oak tree is known for its greatness due to its large size and long lifespan. Some oaks have been known to grow to 100 feet tall and live for well over 200 years. Oaks also develop acorns that feed several animals and replant more trees. Birds like woodpeckers also enjoy acorns, burying any they can't eat to store them for later. They remember where most of them are, but any left behind has a chance to grow into the new oak tree.

A single giant oak tree can produce nearly ten thousand acorns during the reproductive season.

However, oak trees do not bear fruit yearly; some acorns require up to 18 months to mature. Compared to the amount of fruit they develop, we should recognize that our fruit is lacking.

This is shown by how many are walking in a lost state, far from Christ.

Oak trees are known for their strength and resilience and are often used to symbolize strength, endurance, and wisdom. Oak trees can withstand intense storms, such as hurricanes and tornadoes, and even survive without leaves.

Oak trees often grow slowly, allowing them to develop a sturdy and vigorous framework over time. Their deep root systems provide stability, and their adaptability to various environmental conditions further contributes to their strength, allowing them to withstand harsh weather, diseases, and other challenges.

As Christians, we can conquer the diversities that move into our lives, although we may face many difficulties as we travel down that road of faith. Consider that we are not traveling alone; our Lord and Savior are always with us.

Isaiah 61:3

> O, grant those who mourn in Zion, Giving them a garland instead of ashes, The oil of gladness instead of mourning, The mantle of praise instead of a spirit of fainting. So, they will be called oaks of righteousness, The planting of the Lord, that He may be glorified.

Amid their mourning, the Lord gave them the image of a tree. From the beginning of creation, a tree has been a symbol of life. God shows us how, in our brokenness, God reminds us through Isaiah that we have a new life and can have joy in Him.

The fact that God has compared Christians to an oak is a great honor and a joy. The power of Christ lives in the believer and walks with us through any circumstance. Each of us has the hope that we can stand firm and stand up with certainty.

Think of it this way: the oak tree stands tall in the landscape, mighty and enduring. Similarly, in biblical times, folks looked at these trees and saw a reflection of strength, stability, and resilience. As we journey through the scriptures, these trees are kind of like signals, highlighting moments of spiritual importance.

People are looking for something in the world to give them hope of overcoming the difficulties surrounding them. Many are trying to serve false gods and ideas. History has taught us that there is no satisfaction within that type of worship. When someone looks at that giant oak, they see endurance. They should see the same thing in a Christian walking with the Lord.

Christians walking by faith will lead many to seek their reason for that faith. That opens the door for the introduction to salvation. Once you see their interest, the next step is found in your Bible.

Matthew 28:19–20

"Go therefore and make disciples of all the nations, baptizing them in the name of the Father and of the Son and of the Holy Spirit, teaching them to observe all things that I have commanded you; and lo, I am with you always, even to the end of the age." Amen.

Galatians 6:2

Bear one another's burdens, and so fulfill the law of Christ.

Happiness comes from the love that believers share within and outside their group. Christians want everyone to know that there is a better life through Christ. The children of God are to imitate His love for the world and for those who live in it. When other people see this excitement, they want to be a part of it.

If we do not help others, we are not obeying God's Word. We aren't only supposed to read the Bible but to do what it tells us is the right path to heaven. Doing that will help lead others to salvation through our Lord Jesus Christ.

> This assent to or belief in the truth received upon the divine testimony has always associated with it a deep sense of sin, a distinct view of Christ, a consenting will, and a loving heart, together with a reliance on, a trusting in, or resting in Christ. It is that state of mind in which a poor sinner, conscious of his sin, flees from his guilty self to Christ, his Savior, and rolls over the burden of all his sins on Him. It consists chiefly not in the assent given to the testimony of God in His Word but in embracing with fiducial reliance and trust the one and only Savior whom God reveals. This trust and reliance is of the essence of faith. By faith, the believer directly and immediately appropriates Christ as his own. Faith in its direct act makes Christ ours. It is not a work that God graciously accepts instead of perfect obedience, but is only the hand by which we take hold of the person and work of our Redeemer as the only ground of our salvation.[2]

As the oak tree continues looking for water to ensure future growth, we, as Christians, should continue to focus on the Word of God for our growth. Through the influence of the Holy Spirit, we will receive daily guidance that directs each step closer to our Lord, allowing us to thrive before a lost and dying world that is looking for a new way of life. We should also remember to speak to God daily to increase our relationship with Him. Communication is the key to a closer and much more unified relationship.

---

2. Easton Bible Dictionary.

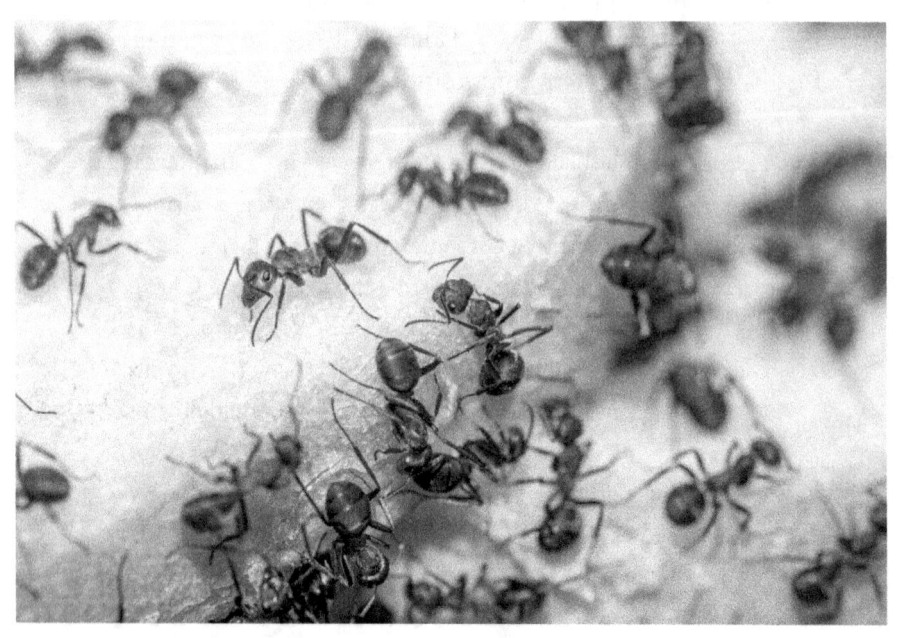

Chapter 5

Observing the Ants

Once, in a dense forest, a single ant wandered alone, struggling to find food. It ventured far but found nothing. Meanwhile, deep within the forest's heart was a colony of army ants marching as one. Together, they were unstoppable.

They crossed rivers, scaled trees, and found more food than any ant could ever hope to gather. Every ant had a role to play, and none acted alone. One day, the wandering ant stumbled upon this colony.

It marveled at their unity and strength and how none sought to outdo the other. Instead, they worked in harmony, guided by a common purpose. The lone ant, weary of its isolation, joined them. Soon, it learned that the ants could overcome obstacles far more significant than anyone could face alone by working together. With the colony, it was no longer lost or weak; it was part of something far more substantial.

Proverbs 6:6–8

Go to the ant, you sluggard! Consider her ways and be wise,
Which, having no captain,

Overseer or ruler, provides her supplies in the summer and gathers her food in the harvest.

Without a commanding officer or any supervisor, the creator provides an ant with the ability to plan. It gathers supplies in the summer and food at harvest time. Ants are ready for winter. They are not surprised. And they do not have a calendar.

The ant takes personal responsibility and does its part in preparing the entire colony for future changes that could cause a short food supply. This example can teach us to be ready for future difficulties. As Christians, we know there will be times when we will need to use the Word of God to fight several battles.

As the ants get ready, so should a child of God. Why don't the seasons when supplies are scarce?

Ants teach us how to be self-motivated. *"Which, having no captain, overseer, or ruler, provides her supplies in the summer, and gathers her food in the harvest"* (Prov 6:7-8). No one carries a whip behind the ant to ensure the work gets done. There are no time cards in the anthill. No ant mothers nag their babies to get out of bed. These creatures are self-motivated and need no captain to ensure they get their work done. Why? Their job is for their own good! As Christians, maturity means we no longer need someone standing behind us, with the Bible in hand, to ensure our work gets done, our moral purity is not compromised, or that we continue to assemble with the saints.[1]

---

1. Chuck D. Pierce, Rebecca Wagner Sytsema, "The Future War of The Church" VDOC.PUB Library.

Colossians 3:23

*And whatever you do, do it heartily, as to the Lord and not
to men.*

This verse implies desire and passion to show that a good
work attitude can reach out in a way that will influence others.
It also suggests that one should work with Christ-like character,
honesty, diligence, integrity, and humility.

This verse explores the idea of setting one's mind on things
above, which can help us experience the joy that God wants to
give us. It also suggests that when one sets his eyes on God, he
can better serve Him.

Ants are well-organized and disciplined in their routes as
they work. Christians should be organized and keep their spiritual dedication. Christians should value others above themselves and work for the interests of others.

Sometimes, in the church setting, Christians have problems
accepting their roles in the body; we forget each one has a
specific job to do. The Bible explains our church as a body of
believers.

Now, the army ants have a scent they leave when looking
for food. When they find food, they return to the colony to let
them know. The scent will lead them to the food and back to
the colony. As they are coming and going, sometimes, they get
knocked off the trail. When this happens, the ants who have
lost their sense of direction rely on their scent. This is called an
ant death spiral, wherein ants follow each other in an endless
circle. They do this until they somehow manage to break out or,
unfortunately, die of exhaustion. The ant death spiral is otherwise known as the ant mill.

Just as the ants lose their ability to stay on the right path
and their sense of direction, we, as Christians, can do the same

thing. If we walk away from the path of the Bible that has directed us through the Holy Spirit, we may be lost.

If God is the ground of all truth, then whatever truths we know, bear witness to Him. Recognizing this, Augustine of Hippo (354-430) constructed an argument for God's existence from our knowledge of truth (*On Free Will*, ii). The mind apprehends certain universal and necessary truths that cannot change, including logical truths like "A is either B or non-B," and mathematical truths. They are neither made true nor amended by the mind as if they were its inferiors; rather, the mind willingly submits to being corrected and judged by them, as by its superiors. Truth exists independently of the mind and is superior to it. The mind fluctuates in its apprehension of truth, but truth remains forever the same. What accounts for its eternal, changeless, and universal status? Individual truths must participate in truth-itself, the eternal and changeless God "in whom and by whom are all things."

Augustine's argument reflects his transformation of the Platonic theory of forms into a theistic context. There are no longer self-subsistent archetypes unified in the Form of the Good. The forms now are eternal truths (*rationes aeternae*) subsisting in the mind of God, for whom all truth is one. They may still be known by recollection, for Augustine also adapts the Platonic theory of innate ideas and dialectical method, but any truth that men grasp is due to the

Logos "who teaches within," enlightening every man who comes into the world (*Concerning the Teacher*, and *Soliloquies*).[2]

---

2. *The Soliloquies of St. Augustine,* translated into English by Rose Elizabeth Cleveland. (Boston: Little, Brown, and Co., 1910).

Christians sometimes lose their view of direction as they lose sight of where they are headed. Unfortunately, like the ants, they continue in a circle, not realizing they are going nowhere. The end is destruction, looking to the world for the right way, which they will not find. The only hope would be if they return to Christ, repent, and return to the right path. Otherwise, they will end up in the circle of death, the second death.

The secret is to do our best to stay on the right path. God's Word, prayer, and fellowship with each other are the answers to staying on the right road to success. By viewing their activities and applying their capabilities to our lives, we can become more established, efficient, and successful. From working together for the greater good to never giving up, ants can provide valuable insight into how to live our lives more effectively.

Romans 8:28

And we know that all things work together for good to those who love God, to those who are the called according to His purpose.

The key to understanding what Paul tells the church in Rome is that we cannot work apart. In the first century, churches were just being established, and starting congregations was difficult.

There were Jewish believers alongside pagans who became Christians. They each had their way of worshiping, and Paul tried to introduce the proper way to get together.

The Bible will be the Christians' daily food. Like the ants, we should know how much we need. We should never forget that there will be dry times on our walk. We must study enough to get us through those changing times. Not only will this help us, but it will also help us to draw closer to Christ. This church had no apostles to come and teach them the functions of the church, and they were trying to do the right things with different opinions. We do not need to be divided.

Most believe that the beginning of this church was from those baptized on the day of Pentecost. They were baptized and learned what they could from the apostles. They took back that knowledge and started a church. Paul believed they were excited and willing to serve the Lord, except there were too many beliefs. This caused much confusion among the congregation. That is precisely what they were trying to avoid. Unlike the ants, they were not working together, causing much confusion.

We should help others walk with us in times of need. Studying God's Word together increases our growth. The ants work together; without their dedication to one another, their journey would fail.

Another thing we can learn from the ants is that they search for their needs. As Christians, we need to read the Bible and search the scriptures. That means studying to the best of our ability. You can use concordances and commentaries to help with your research.

The main goal is to be prepared for what the enemy may throw at you. Know the tricks and lies of the Devil, for he is doing everything within his power to stop Christians from succeeding in their walk. We are told to be on the watch for the enemy who does not want us to make it or to help others enjoy their faith.

Another main point we can learn from the ants is that they work until they die. There is no room to stop in the middle of our walk in faith. It won't be until death that we will receive our reward. Realizing it was through our determination that made heaven possible.

Ants often teach people beneficial lessons, showing us the power of teamwork, cooperation, self-discipline, and perseverance. Watching them work together encourages us to stay focused on our goals and never give up.

From hard work and commitment to teamwork and communication, ants demonstrate some of the most essential principles of life that we can all learn from. They are known for their energy and often work long hours to ensure survival. This proves that success is possible through hard work and dedication.

We can also learn from ants that cooperation is the key. The ants' determination and persistence can be a great example to us. Watching them work together can inspire us to stay focused on our goals and never give up. Ants also show the value of supply organization, being efficient with their supplies and ensuring each does its part to ensure the colony's success. Ants remind us that we can all influence regardless of size. They show us that even the smallest creatures can have a big effect and that we should never underestimate our ability to do our part.

Ants remain focused and dedicated to the task; they never get preoccupied. We can use this in any goal or job; staying focused and dedicated is essential. Ants are very quick to change in their surroundings. We can apply this characteristic to our lives; adjusting and correcting changes is essential.

When *The Star-Spangled Banner* is sung at sporting events, the climactic phrase comes to an elongated high note: "O'er the land of the freeee ...." The cheers begin here. Even though the song goes on to talk about "the brave," this is an afterthought. Both the melody line and our culture highlight freedom as *the* main theme and value of our society.

Freedom has come to be defined as the absence of any

limitations or constraints on us. By this definition, the fewer boundaries we have on our choices and actions, the freer we feel ourselves to be. Held in this form, I want to argue that the narrative has gone wrong and is doing damage. Modern freedom is the freedom of self-assertion. I am free if I may do whatever I want. But defining freedom this way ... is unworkable because it is an impossibility .... We need some kind of moral norms and constraints on our actions if we are to live together.[3]

---

3. Tim Keller, "Freedom Has Become the Ultimate Good Society," *Christianity Today*, 2024.

Chapter 6

The Wonder of the Bees

A hive of honeybees was in a vast meadow. Each had a role: the queen bee provided guidance, the worker bees gathered nectar, and the drones stood ready to support the hive.

Each bee contributed to the greater good of the colony. Together, they produced sweet honey and ensured the hive's survival. One day, a young worker bee became tired of its role, believing it was too small to have influence. It looked at the flowers it visited and thought, "What does it matter if I skip a few today?"

The hive is significant, and many others can do this work. So, it rested while the other bees continued their labor. Over time, more bees saw the young worker bee's example and thought the same. Little by little, fewer flowers were visited, and the supply of nectar grew scarce.

They returned to the flowers, working tirelessly to restore the hive's strength. Once again, the honey flowed, and the bees thrived, united by a common purpose. Like the honeybee, we have a role in God's plan. No matter how small our efforts seem, they contribute to the greater good. When we work together, each fulfilling our purpose, we create something far sweeter than we could alone.

Bees have been seen as illustrations for Christians in several ways, particularly through their qualities and behaviors that reflect biblical principles. Bees are known for their hard work and dedication to the hive. Similarly, Christians must be diligent in their faith and service to others and serve the Lord. Our dedication comes through prayer and Bible study.

Colossians 3:23–24

And whatever you do, do it heartily, as to the Lord and not to me, knowing that from the Lord you will receive the reward of the inheritance; for you serve the Lord.

Whatever you do, work at it with all your heart, as working for the Lord, not for human masters: community and unity. Bees work together in harmony for the common good of the hive, like the Christian community, and are designed to function as one body united in Christ.

Bees spread life by pollinating plants, enabling them to grow and bear fruit. Similarly, Christians are called to spread the Gospel's good news, helping others grow in faith and bear spiritual fruit.

Bees are known to defend their hive from intruders. This can represent Christians being protective of their faith and standing firm in the face of challenges. A bee's life is often self-sacrifice for the good of the hive, a call to selflessness, and to put others above themselves. God's children are called to live in harmony with God's design. They are matching the sacrificial love of Christ.

Pollination and spreading the Gospel. Bees spread life by pollinating plants, enabling them to grow and bear fruit. Similarly, Christians will spread the Gospel's good news, helping others grow in faith and bear spiritual fruit—protection of the hive.

The honeybee's actual architectural skill and expertise are demonstrated by the beauty of the honeycomb, its structural strength, and the speed with which they construct the uniform hexagonal cells. The building of the comb is accomplished first by "plastering" the wax into an estimated position in the form of round cells.

Then, the wax walls are thinned to a uniform thickness to produce the hexagonal cells for strength and saving of wax. As nutritionists, they prepare one kind of food for the queen larvae and another for the worker and drone larvae. Each larva receives approximately 10,000 visits from the nurse bees during development.

Like other insects, honeybees are cold-blooded and have a body temperature close to that of their environment. However, working as a single organism, the honeybee colony can maintain uniform hive temperatures under northern winter conditions identical to those in summer or the tropics.

The most apparent trait dominant in honeybees is their great industry. Honeybees do not procrastinate by doing tomorrow what they can do now. The bees that gather this food do not live long enough to enjoy it. The bees must be productive in gathering enough food and training so many young bees.

The lesson here is that they work hard and do not get to enjoy the benefits. Christians should work hard and stay in prayer. We may not see the final stage of our work and those we lead to the Lord, but one day comes when God's children reap from their excellent work.

Honeybees use the position of the sun and time to determine the direction they are flying and the distance from their hive. By the position of the sun, bees know what time it is.

They also use the position and angle of the sun to the horizon to navigate and fly in a straight line. Just as the honeybee flies in a straight line, Christians should take this lesson as a reminder to focus on Christ. Wavering in different directions will only lead in an unknown direction. In many cases, Christians will end up lost, not even knowing how they ended up in that situation.

First, the young bees must learn to fly and position themselves to avoid getting lost once they leave the hive. Three-week-old bees leave the hives in groups, flying in ever-increasing sweeps back and forth around the front of the hive, learning the look and location of it so they can find their way home later.

Proverbs 22:6

> Train up a child in the way he should go, and when he is old, he will not depart from it.

Today, children are left to grow up without substantial training, especially when teaching them the way of the Lord. Few parents develop a daily Bible study and pray with the entire family. We are too busy to take time for God, yet in disaster circumstances, families always find time for God. This is a false indication that God is more like a spare tire; you only need Him when there is trouble. The honeybees know how important it is to teach their young bees how to live.

Older honeybees know of the dangers away from the protective beehive. We, as adults, are aware of the risks in this world where everything seems okay. That is how we become blinded by the excitement of living in sin. We must teach our children from the view of God's Word.

Proverbs 14:12

There is a way that seems right to a man, but its end is the way of death.

Older bees, particularly in honeybee colonies, teach younger bees through a social learning process. They often pass down behavioral knowledge about the dividing line of labor. Younger bees start as "nurse" bees, caring for larvae and cleaning the hive. Older bees provide signals as they grow, and the young bees switch roles like searching for pollen and nectar.

Young bees learn by interacting with older bees, observing their behavior, and participating in communal tasks. The hive's cooperative structure encourages learning through experience, where younger bees gradually take on more complicated roles as they age.

Older bees help the younger bees learn survival skills, hive duties, and foraging through observation, communication, and chemical signals. This reflects a deep interconnectedness and cooperation essential for the hive's survival:

We will not have a godly home if the Lord does not lead our churches. They will not provide a place that will spiritually nourish the community. Instead, the church will be another place to gather. This situation is devastating to the Kingdom of God. Christians must wake up and remember that we should build up the church.

The honeybees have no interest in the rest of the world. They are only interested in what God created them to do—nothing more. If only those who have accepted Christ as their Savior would acknowledge that they are now living for Him and not themselves.

Effective church growth is designed to attract new

members, engage the existing congregation, and create a community that fosters spiritual development. These strategies can include outreach programs.

To gain help from our congregation, they must first see the need. Many people are comfortable with what they have, not realizing the lack of interaction with the community.

The prominent people in the church are outside in a world of exciting scenes of sin. The Lord's Church members are symbols like bees; they know what their work is, and they do it.

When new visitors come to our church, we may inadvertently overlook the challenges a visitor might encounter. Taking a step back allows us to identify areas where we can enhance the guests' experience and make them feel genuinely valued. This is one way we can be effective in our community.

The personality of the honeybee goes beyond my deepest thoughts. This small creation is doing precisely what they were created to do. What happens to humans? They have left God and His plan for an adventure deep into the sins of this world. We know that heaven and earth shall pass away. Why hold on to something that will not last?

Matthew 24:35–37

> Heaven and earth will pass away, but My words will not pass away. But of that day and hour, no one knows, not even the angels of heaven, but MY Father only. But as the days of Noah were, so also will the coming of the Son of Man be.

One could emphasize the following key points when reflecting on Christianity and the honeybee. The honeybee, dedicated to community, work, and productivity, illustrates the Christian life just as the honeybee works tirelessly for the benefit of the hive. Christians are called to work for the benefit of the body of Christ and the church and to serve others selflessly.

The bee's ability to transform pollen into honey can symbolize how Christians, through faith and obedience to God, can transform challenges or trials into spiritual fruits, such as love, joy, and peace. Additionally, the honeybee's instinct to gather and store food in preparation for winter can reflect the Christian's call to prepare spiritually by storing up treasures in heaven and staying rooted in God's Word, preparing for eternity with Christ.

Timothy 6:12

Fight the good fight of faith, lay hold on eternal life, to which you were also called, and have confessed the good confession in the presence of many witnesses.

When we look at the situation around us, it may not be what we expected. Things might seem overwhelming sometimes, and many people try to take it in and manage it. The bees seem to adapt and keep doing what they learn from nature.

As Christians, we must learn to walk by our faith in Christ, knowing that it might not seem pleasant then. Trusting that He knows what is best, I always tell everyone, including myself, that everything in this world is temporary. There is no need to fret about something you know will disappear soon.

As we walk by faith, not sight, this chaotic world will not take us away from God. Just knowing everything we see is temporary makes life's journey more enduring. We must look up and realize that we will fall somewhere away from this earth one day.

Chapter 7

The Magnificat Butterfly

A caterpillar crawled on the ground in a quiet meadow, content with its simple life of eating leaves and staying close to the earth. It lived with no understanding of what lay ahead. One day, an inner call urged it to stop, build a cocoon, and remain still.

The caterpillar obeyed without fully understanding why. Days passed, and a transformation took place in the cocoon's stillness. When the time was right, the cocoon broke open, and a beautiful, vibrant, and accessible butterfly emerged.

Where once it had crawled, it now soared, seeing the world from new heights. The butterfly was not born for the ground but for the skies. Its wings were always meant to carry it, though it had to go through a time of waiting and transformation to realize its purpose.

Like the butterfly, we often go through seasons of waiting or uncertainty, not understanding God's plan. However, if we trust in the process and allow Him to work in our lives, we will emerge transformed, able to see His greater purpose. Just as the caterpillar must trust the cocoon, we must trust God's timing, knowing He is preparing us for something greater.

Before a caterpillar forms its cocoon, it must shed its skin four or five times as it grows. This reveals that shedding old patterns and habits, while painful, is often necessary to achieve growth. Consider how we, as Christians, usually shed certain items that should not be a part of our lives. Sin after sin, most of the time, we are not sure how they got there.

Like the butterfly, we need time alone to recharge! Rather than a physical transformation, however, our time alone is about creating emotional transitions. Taking time alone to decompress and meditate can lead to immense internal growth for us, just as it leads the caterpillar to display its colorful new set of wings!

Sometimes, people are like caterpillars, crawling on the ground through dirt and rubbish, looking for food, and wondering what life has to offer. It is not until this person finds Christ and is reborn by God's Spirit that a new, beautiful life appears, just as the butterfly emerges from its cocoon.

After the butterfly experiences its new life, the old life is forgotten, and the new butterfly flies far above the dirt it used to crawl in. When Jesus comes into our lives, we are washed by the bloodshed on the cross, and we become clean from all the filth we have attained by living in sin. At this point, we, too, fly high above the sins of our past.

This transformation signifies our journey from sin and brokenness to redemption and new life in Christ. Some Christians have just experienced being re-born into Jesus Christ, shedding their old selves and embracing a renewed identity in Him.

The wisdom that believers experience. Just as the butterfly struggles to break free from its cocoon, we, too, face struggles and challenges in our Christian walk. However, these obstacles shape us and strengthen our faith as we rely on God's grace and guidance.

Romans 12:2

And do not be conformed to this world, but be transformed by the renewing of your mind, that you may prove what is that good and acceptable and perfect will of God.

The butterfly descriptions should inspire our hearts to reflect on God's transformative work, leading us to a deeper understanding of spiritual growth and renewal in Him.

Butterflies have several ways of protecting themselves, each offering a lesson we can apply spiritually or personally. Here are a few ways they defend themselves and what we can learn. We can learn to avoid harmful situations by being wise and discerning about where we go and what we engage in, like butterflies using their environment for protection.

Spiritually, this could be about living in position with God's word to avoid what threatens our spiritual health. We can learn from this by accepting wisdom and acting with integrity, reflecting strength and good character. Spiritually, we can mimic Christ, striving to reflect His qualities, which offer protection through faith.

Each aspect of a butterfly's behavior teaches us about awareness, sensitivity, and living with purpose. God's creation equips even the smallest creatures to survive, and we are also given spiritual tools for protection.

By imitating Christ and His character, we protect ourselves spiritually like the butterfly mirrors more dangerous species for safety. More than anything else, guard your heart, for everything you do flows from it. We are called to guard our hearts by setting boundaries based on faith and values.

If we settle in and realize that God's plan is correct, we can learn to trust Him for every aspect of our life. Just like the butterfly who never tries to change their lives, they live it according to the will of God. How much would we gain in living a life for Christ? As Christians, the future is known because we have been informed by God's Word in the Bible that there is a time when all of God's children will be called home.

The butterfly, transforming from a simple caterpillar to a beautiful creature with wings, can teach us great spiritual lessons. Just as the butterfly changes, so too can we be changed by renewing our minds through the work of the Holy Spirit. The process of sanctification in a believer's life mirrors this conversion as we are conformed progressively to the image of Christ.

The butterfly also reminds us of the shortness of life, the concept of a new beginning in Christ, and the promise of resurrection and eternal life. Let us consider these truths and seek to grow spiritually, just as the butterfly experiences an extraordinary change.

2 Corinthians 5:17

Therefore, if anyone is in Christ, he is a new creation; old things have passed away; behold, all things have become new.

When a person turns from their sins and experiences conversion, it often involves an intense inner shift driven by self-mindfulness, conviction, and a desire for spiritual renewal. This change can be seen as a return to a more faithful self, positioning one's life with higher values and truths.

In the middle, there is typically an acknowledgment of wrongs committed and a sense of humility, recognizing the need for grace and forgiveness. The process can be ongoing, marked by small steps of progress rather than instant change.

If God is the ground of all truth, then whatever truths we know bear witness to Him. Recognizing this, Augustine of Hippo (354–430) constructed an argument for God's existence from our knowledge of truth (*On Free Will*, ii). The mind apprehends certain universal and necessary truths that cannot change, including logical truths like "A is either B or non-B," and mathematical truths. They are neither made true nor amended by the mind as if they were its inferiors; rather the mind willingly submits to being corrected and judged by them, as by its superiors. Truth exists independently of the mind and is superior to it. The mind fluctuates in its apprehension of truth, but truth remains forever the same. What accounts for its eternal, changeless, and universal status? Individual truths must participate in Truth-itself, the eternal and changeless God "in whom and by whom are all things."

Augustine's argument reflects his transformation of the Platonic theory of forms into a theistic context. There are no longer self-subsistent archetypes unified in the Form of the Good. The forms now are eternal truths (*rationes aeternae*) subsisting in the mind of God, for whom all truth is one. They may still be known by recollection, for Augustine also adapts the Platonic theory of innate ideas and dialectical method, but any truth that men grasp is due to the Logos "who teaches within," enlightening every man who comes into the world.[1]

It involves renewing the mind, choosing new habits, and often conquering past temptations. Faith plays a significant role in this change, offering strength and a source to build. Through prayer, scripture, and a relationship with God, a person can find guidance and comfort in the transformation process.

Additionally, it is essential to remember that change is not

---

1. Augustine of Hippo. (n.d.) *Free Will* .

just an individual effort but often requires a compassionate society. Support from others can be crucial to staying on the course and growing spiritually.

This is a settled spiritual attitude that small thoughts of sin lead to small thoughts of Christ. We will love little if we think we have been forgiven just a little. The same principle applies, however, to those who have forgotten how much they have been forgiven. And to one degree or another, we are all prone to fail.

So, too, with us. If we are going to love Christ much, we need to remember the depths from which He saved us. If we are going to treasure all we have in Him, we need to remember who we were without Him. In ourselves, we are evil; in God's sight, we are dissatisfying.

Those two facts, taken together, lead us to a third: without Christ, we are hopelessly condemned. The judgment has already begun. Paul writes. The wrath of God is revealed from heaven against all ungodliness and unrighteousness of men.

And how is God revealing his wrath? By handing us over to our favorite sins. "God gave them up in the lusts of their hearts." We desired freedom from God, not realizing that the more distant we are from Him, the more imprisoned we are to sin.

In Christ, we are brought before God in rightness; the provision made for us at Calvary paid the price for our sins.

John Newton famously said on his deathbed, "I am a great sinner, and Christ is a great Savior." The two statements always belong together. If our sin was small, then so is our Savior. But our thoughts of Christ cannot be too great if we were corrupted, displeasing, and condemned.

The butterfly has set forth many examples for humanity to observe, from crawling in the dirt to being reborn into a beautiful creature. Living a life above the ground it used to crawl on. As he looks back, the re-born transition has given him a new view of the world.

From the losses of sin to the uplifting from the Spirit of God, these people experienced a new life filled with joy and peace of mind. They were no longer sunk in sin but succeeded in being closer to the one who saved them. Knowing your name is in the Book of Life is plenty to shout about.

The butterfly used to crawl in the mud of life as I had in my earlier years. And just as it went through a new birth, so did I. The butterfly sailed off above the mud it used to crawl in. I rose above the sin that had me tied up, and the grace of God turned me loose. Now, I can also look at where I have come from. Praise the Lord!

Psalms 1:6

For the LORD knows the way of the righteous, But the way of the ungodly shall perish.

Just as the butterfly does not stop once it spreads its wings, our spiritual journey does not end with conversion. Every day is an encouragement to grow, to trust God more deeply, and to replicate His beauty in the world around us. The butterfly teaches us that change is not once; but an ongoing process guided by the same Creator who designed its extraordinary journey.

James 1:22–25

But be doers of the word, and not hearers only, deceiving yourselves. For if anyone is a hearer of the word and not a doer, he is like a man observing his natural face in a mirror, for he observes himself, goes away, and immediately forgets what kind of man he was. But he who investigates the perfect law of liberty and continues in it. And is not a forgetful hearer but a doer of the work; this one will be blessed in what he does.

Chapter 8

The Incredible Spider

There was once a spider that lived in a cornfield. She was a giant spider and had spun a beautiful web between the corn stalks. She got fat eating all the flies caught in the web. She liked her home and planned to stay there for the rest of her life.

One day, the spider caught a little fly in her web, and just as the spider was about to eat him, the fly said, "If you let me go, I will tell you something important that will save your life." The spider paused for a moment and listened because she was amused.

"You better get out of this cornfield," the little fly said, "The harvest is coming!" The spider smiled and said, "What is this harvest you are discussing? You are just telling me a story." But the little fly said, "Oh no, it is true. The owner of this field is coming to harvest it soon. All the stalks will be knocked down, and the corn will be gathered. The giant machines will kill you if you stay here." The spider said, "I do not believe in harvests and huge machines that knock down corn stalks. How can you prove this?"

The little fly continued, "Just look at the corn. See how it is planted in rows? It proves an intelligent designer created this field." The spider laughed and mockingly said, "This field has evolved and has nothing to do with a creator. Corn always grows that way."

The fly went on to explain, "Oh no! This field belongs to the owner who planted it, and the harvest is coming soon." The spider grinned and said to the little fly, "I don't believe you," then the spider ate the fly for lunch.

A few days later, the spider was laughing about the story the little bug had told him. He thought to himself, "A harvest! What a silly idea. I have lived here all my life, and nothing has ever disturbed me. I have been here since these stalks were just a foot off the ground, and I'll be here for the rest of my life because nothing will ever change in this field. Life is good, and I have it made."

The next day was a beautiful sunny day in the cornfield. The sky above was clear, and there was no wind at all. As the spider was about to nap that afternoon, she noticed thick, dusty clouds moving toward her. She could hear the roar of a great engine and said, "I wonder what that could be?"

The webs of deceit and sin are easily torn apart, just as an innocent hand can destroy a spider's web. The spider's web compares human systems' passing and unreliable nature when separated from God.

In a quiet garden, a spider carefully weaves its web, each strand meticulously placed to form an intricate design. Day after day, the spider works, spinning and repairing, never tiring of its task. Though invisible to the eye, the web is strong enough to catch the spider's survival needs. Yet, despite the web's perfection, one strong gust of wind or careless passerby can instantly destroy it.

But the spider does not despair. Without hesitation, it

begins to weave again, knowing that each web is temporary, but its purpose endures.

It is said that we always have spiders within a few feet of us. Some people find them scary, but the world would be overrun with flies and insects without them. I wonder how many spiders are killed each day by those who are frightened of them. Some people think they are dirty bugs living in messy homes, but even Buckingham Palace has many spiders.

They do not mind living in rich or poor houses because, in every situation, the spider will spin a web. Solomon spoke of her because of the magnificent web she weaves. Who taught her to do this? God gave her the wisdom when He created her.

Believers are everywhere, but few are productive in the Lord's work. God has given each of us the ability to call the lost to Christ, but most of us hold back because we do not want to offend anyone. Jesus told us to go and share the good news with the world.

The Bible speaks of the negative aspects of the spider. The spider's web is extraordinary. It is extremely weak and can be broken by the slightest touch, yet it is strong enough to catch even giant insects. The wicked are clever enough to use every means available to destroy the spirit, soul, and body of every man, woman, and child. They spend time and effort getting the job done. They do not realize that they are doing the work of the devil.

One warm summer afternoon, a spider was noticed weaving its web between the branches of an oak tree. The silk reflected in the sunlight, delicate and shimmering. The web seemed fragile, something a gust of wind could quickly destroy.

The spider worked carefully, unaware of anyone's presence, creating a home and a trap. A small fly buzzed into the web, caught in the silky trap. The web, which seemed so fragile moments ago, held firm. The spider swiftly moved in, using what it had built for survival.

> God's compassions: they have so long sinned against mercy that they have now quite sinned it away. His eye shall not spare, neither will he have pity. Nay, his justice being glorified in their ruin, he will be pleased with it, though now he would rather they should turn and live. Ah! I will ease me of my adversaries.
>
> Now God is ready to hear their prayers and to meet them with mercy, if they would but seek to him for it; but then the door will be shut, and they shall cry in vain. "Then shall they call upon me when it is too, late, Lord.[1]

It shows how fragile our lives can be without a foundation rooted in Christ. Just as it patiently weaves its web, God weaves His plan through every aspect of life, even those we do not fully understand. The uncertainty of the web is deceiving. Though it may look weak, it perfectly matches the spider's needs. I have heard that spider silk is stronger than steel, which is the same thickness.

Finding purpose in the spider's web and our lives is part of a larger design. Often, we go through difficult or uneasy events that feel wobbly or unstable. These moments may make us examine God's purpose. But just as the spider spins its web in planning, God uses those opposing times to shape us and fulfill His greater plan.

The spider does not question why it must spin its web; it simply operates according to its design. In the same way, we are called to trust that God's design, even in seasons of doubt, is for

---

1. Matthew Henry, *Commentary of the Whole Bible.* (1706). (p.2599/5414).

our good. The trials that seem like webs of struggles often prepare us for growth, wisdom, and a deeper bond with God.

Just as the spider's web plays a fundamental role in nature, the difficulties and unexpected challenges in our lives are part of God's divine stability. What we may originally fear or reject often holds a hidden blessing, influencing us into who we are meant to be.

We could combine the idea of spiders into this book by showing how even unsettling or undesirable creatures serve an inspired design in the natural world, much like opposing or unpleasant incidents can lead to spiritual growth.

It is amazing how God works in the world. We cannot see how much God is doing. If we doubt Him, it is easy to think He is inactive. But God is certainly working for our benefit. If we look for His Glory at the right time, we will see it in all His creations.

Everything is part of God's greater purpose. We can find beauty and purpose even in what initially seems unattractive. This might confirm how even unwanted creatures like spiders play a part in the divine balance of nature.

Some people are frightened of spiders, and they won't go near them. Others think they are ugly and make them shiver, so they kill them. But spiders are very wonderful and clever. If you look closely at their webs, you cannot help but be amazed.

I want to tell you about a spider that saved a man's life. This happened during a terrible time in history. King Charles IX of France did not like the Huguenots, who were Christians. On Saint Bartholomew's Day in 1572, he ordered, "Kill them all so that not a single one be left to reproach me!" Thousands of Huguenots were killed before it all ended.

One man who was saved was a baker. King Charles's

soldiers were hunting for him with orders to kill him because they knew he was a Christian.

The baker knew they were hunting for him, so he climbed into his big oven, which was not heated that day, and closed the door on himself. As soon as he did, God sent a little spider along to help him. This little spider spun a web all over the oven door.

When the soldiers searched the bakehouse, one of them suggested that the baker might be hiding in the oven. But another soldier said, "No man, he is not in there. Don't you see the spider's web all over the door?" To them, the spider's web meant that the oven door had not been opened for quite a while. So, they went away without opening the oven door, and the baker safely escaped.[2]

On the other hand, the spider's web represents a trap. There are many ways a person can end up trapped in something that seemed so risk-free. The world is deceiving and will attract you according to your flaws. Growing into spiritual maturity and taking on the nature of Jesus does not ease the attraction of sin. Satan's tempting attractions often come in innocent ways that may catch us off guard. Thank goodness God's blessings keep us on the narrow path to heaven. This battle between flesh and spirit is ongoing, so how can we escape or avoid the devil's trap?

The desires of the human flesh and its sensual desires are part of the war between flesh and spirit. One of the devil's traps, common to all people, is how we respond to being hurt, insulted, or not getting our way. It is no wonder that disagreements and arguments stem from our self-interest, the ugly old monster of pride.

---

2. This is a folk tale often shared in sermons.

C.S. Lewis, in his book *Mere Christianity*, points out that,

the utmost evil is pride. Unchastity, anger, greed, drunken-ness, and all that, are mere fleabites in comparison: it was through pride that the devil became the devil: Pride leads to every other vice: it is the complete anti-God state of mind.[3]

Learning of Scripture will guard against abuse and false teaching. It will also expand the ability to conquer pride's self-interest and yield the role of humility, like that of Jesus.

Humility yields to God and submits an angry tongue to kindness. Humility serves God's purposes first.

Reacting to difficulties hurts, disagreements, and insults provide spiritual compliance with the Lord and confirms the purity of heart and holiness of character.

2 Timothy 2:22

Flee also youthful lusts; but pursue righteousness, faith, love, peace with those who call on the Lord out of a pure heart.

When you come in from working out in the yard, you can see how dirty you have gotten. How are you going to get cleaned up? You will probably use water and soap in the house. God provided the blood of Jesus to cleanse us from all sins. That is why we are clean when we trust Christ as our Savior and baptize in His name.

The secret to not falling into the devil's trap is to remain established in the Word of God. Starting each day in prayer for forgiveness and direction. Ponder on those things that relate to God, not being surpassed by the bright lights of sin.

---

3. C. S. Lewis, *Mere Christianity*, (New York: HarperCollins, 1952).

James 1:14

> *Then, when desire has conceived, it gives birth to sin; and sin, when it is full-grown, brings forth death.*

Chapter 9

Why the Snail?

The Snail's Journey** Once upon a time, in a lush green forest, all the creatures prepared for a great gathering on the tallest hill. The wise owl announced that there would be a grand feast where the first to arrive would receive the greatest prize of all: the gift of understanding. The news spread quickly, and the fastest animals—the deer, the hare, and the eagle—set off immediately, confident they would arrive before all others.

But among the creatures, there was also a humble snail. Though he moved slowly, he was determined to make the journey. "Why even bother?" the hare laughed, zipping past him.

"You will never make it in time!" The deer, too, shook her head. "It's a waste of effort. Turn back now." But the snail kept moving forward, inch by inch, with unwavering focus. Every day, the other animals mocked his slow progress.

But the snail persisted, never losing sight of his goal. Days turned into weeks, and though the others had long since reached the top, the snail continued his climb.

Finally, after a long and challenging journey, he arrived at the feast. To his surprise, the wise owl was still there, waiting. "You have arrived, my little friend," the owl said kindly.

"The greatest prize is not only for those who are swift but for those who persevere." The snail looked around and saw that many who had arrived first were no longer present, having grown impatient and left. The owl gave the snail the gift of understanding, and the snail learned that life's greatest treasures are found not in speed but in steadfastness and patience.

Galatians 6:9

And let us not grow weary while doing good, for in due season we shall reap if we do not lose heart.

Sometimes, life lessons can be problematic; However, we must understand that the Lord will see that we will one day enter heaven. Rushing sometimes causes us to overlook the main attributes of life. An old, wise thought someone once said could inspire us (Stop and smell the roses), help us enjoy life better, and help us realize that God wants us to depend on Him.

Snails move slowly but consistently. Their calculated pace can indicate the importance of patience in spiritual growth. Like the snail, we do not always need to rush. We make the most progress in faith when we move progressively, trusting God's timing.

A snail carries its home on its back, always protected. This can serve as a reminder of our security in God's presence. No matter where we go or what we face, we can carry our faith with us like a spiritual shelter.

Snails are small, humble creatures that are easily ignored. They symbolize the spiritual benefit of humility. Like the snail, we are called to live humbly, realizing that true greatness comes from God in the love that flows through our hearts, not outward appearances.

Snails can thrive in different environments by changing their pace and conduct. Spiritually, this can reveal the importance of flexibility and trust in God when traveling through life's encounters. As they move forward, snails leave a trail behind, representing their effort to conquer the opposition. This mirrors our spiritual journeys, where perseverance in the face of obstacles leaves behind a testimony of faith and endurance.

Christians should be walking faithfully with the Lord, not being persuaded by the pace of the world but staying steadfast in their spiritual journey. We can learn about the importance of spiritual protection. Just as the shell shields the snail from harm, we are called to put on the whole armor of God to guard ourselves against the schemes of the evil one. Let us be alert of the snail's lessons about endurance and protection.

One important life lesson from the snails is persistence and perseverance. We need to stay committed and determined, even when our progress is slow. The snail's flexibility reminds us that success is not always instant but will come to those who persist till the end.

Snails have long been associated with spiritual insight and inner growth. Their slow pace and gentle nature remind us to take our time in life's journey and understand the beauty around us. They teach us patience, persistence, and the importance of self-care.

Psalm 145:9

The Lord is good to all, And His tender mercies are over all His works.

It does not matter if you are beginning or have lived for the

Lord for years. God's mercy still covers you in each step; accountability is the key to your extent for future success. Consider that many things can distract us from walking with God. This is why sometimes we need to learn from the snail and slow down.

Perseverance is an important character trait that can help us grow in faith and maturity. Jesus uses our struggles to develop and fine-tune our bond with Him. Our battles can point out the weak and vital parts of our faith. We must endure and not give up. The result of perseverance is a firm belief in God's truth and promises. Study and reflect on God's Word, knowing He is with you and will sustain you through every trial.

Remember that your trials are temporary, and dim compared to the eternal blessings God has prepared for you. Reflect on past challenges and difficulties and how God took you through them. Remember His dedication, and let those events feed your endurance in current trials. Gain self-discipline to focus on your goals, even when faced with obstacles and barriers. Stay committed to your faith and persevere in following God's purposes for your life.

God has perfect timing for His plans. Patiently wait for His direction and resource, knowing He works all things together for your good. Perseverance is essential for our spiritual growth and development. By fastening ourselves to God's promises, educating a mindset of joy, seeking support from fellow believers, determined in prayer, focusing on the eternal position, gaining strength from God's presence, learning from past participations, embracing growth and learning, dedicated to self-correction, and concealed in God's timing, we can establish the important quality of perseverance in our own lives.

James 4:8

> *Draw near to God and He will draw near to you. Cleanse your*
> *hands, you sinners, and purify your hearts, you double-minded.*

Perseverance is not an easy journey. It requires strength, resistance to sinful acts, and steady trust in God. But as we improve perseverance, we become more like Christ, who endured the ultimate trials and challenges on our behalf. This is how we can find comfort and inspiration during these trying times.

1 Corinthians 15:57

> *But thanks be to God, who gives us victory through our Lord*
> *Jesus Christ.*

Even when our vision tells us nothing is right, we should focus on faith. Faith is the believing factor in trusting in the Lord, even at times of trouble. Trusting oneself can become a mess; most people do not like cleaning up messes. The best way to prevent this is to lean on the Lord for support.

We must love those things that keep Him in our hearts and minds. We are instructed to behave pleasingly according to His Word, which means that each choice we make should be according to His will.

Revelation 3:5

> *He who overcomes shall be clothed in white garments, and I*
> *will not blot out his name from the Book of Life, but I will*
> *confess his name before My Father and His angels.*

The snail's slowness reflects the idea that he has some-where to go; it may seem to us that the snail will never get there at that speed. Slowness is not a problem in life; it is the ability to complete the journey. Without faith, there is no journey to a fulfilling life because looking at what we see can be devastating.

Let us proceed slowly, learning that Jesus leads the way. We should trust His Word for guidance on our path. The main goal in life is our salvation and the salvation of our loved ones. Seeking those things that isolated us from the Lord will affect not only our lives but also the lives of those who are looking to us for direction.

Despite their slow pace of life, snails impact our planet's systems. Whether enriching soil fertility or balancing food chains, these tiny creatures embrace significant roles within their humble existence. Snails offer rich symbolic meanings across diverse civilizations and cycles. Their attributes teach lessons on life's journey, flexibility, and inner strength.

Psalm 145:14

The LORD upholds all who fall and raises up all who are bowed down.

Some people believe that a slower life is possible but fear that they will miss out if they do not keep up the pace. So, they bend to the pressure and miss the gift of rest and slowness. If you look around where you live, everything is in a hurry. Sometimes, we cannot fit everything in because there is so much and little time.

Isaiah 40:31

But those who wait on the LORD shall renew their strength;
They shall mount up with wings like eagles, they shall run and
not be weary, they shall walk and not faint.

Battles come in all shapes and sizes; fears, addictions, persecution, and worries can all seem to take over our thoughts. God tells us that we will face trials but should not lose hope! We should be reassured that God has called you an overcomer!

Snails encourage us to savor each moment, understanding that every step impacts our life's journey, no matter how small.

A snail's shell is its primary defense system, providing shelter from external threats. Spiritually, this can represent the inner strength and resistance we all possess. Just as the snail moves away to its shell for safety, we, too, can turn inwards, utilizing our inner resources when faced with life's challenges. As Christians, we can always turn to our Lord for guidance and shelter in dealing with the enemy.

Snails have extremely sensitive tentacles that help them detect changes in their situation. This physical trait indicates the importance of instinct and spiritual awareness. We can better navigate our path by tuning into our inner senses and realizing the occasions and challenges ahead.

Being aware of our surroundings is an essential importance in life. Sadly, it is easy to become preoccupied. Sinful actions are very tempting and can lead to lustful actions. We must walk looking accompanied by our faith in God. He will never put you in a position that makes sinful actions.

Psalm 119:133

Direct my steps by Your word, and let no iniquity have dominion over me.

1 Thessalonians 5:22

Abstain from every form of evil.

How most people would react to this verse is easier said than done, realizing those inward yearnings. Sin is beautiful to most people. It accomplishes exactly what it aimed for in that outcome. The enemy will continue to overshadow us with all those various temptations. He seeks to lead as many as he can away from the Lord; he wants all of us to be destroyed in the same way he will be.

As the snail is familiar with its surroundings, so should the Christian be. We know from what we have learned through our daily Bible studies. Studying the Bible with continual prayer will grow our faith in God and our understanding of sin. With this lifestyle, our progress will lead to a closer walk with God. The closer we get, the brighter our light becomes.

Chapter 10

The Amazing Dragonfly

Once, in a small pond, a group of water bugs lived peacefully beneath the surface. They spent their days crawling on the mud at the bottom, unaware of the world above. One by one, the bugs would occasionally climb up the long stems of the plants and disappear.

The others, left behind, would wonder what happened to their friends but were too afraid to climb and find out for themselves. One day, a young water bug named Lani made a promise to her friends.

"If I ever climb one of those stems, I will return to tell you what happens!" The others agreed, though deep inside, they doubted whether she could return. Time passed, and one day, Lani felt an irresistible urge to climb. She knew this was the moment she had promised, so she began her journey up the stem, leaving the familiar waters behind.

As she broke through the pond's surface, she felt the sun's warmth on her back for the first time. Suddenly, something wonderful happened. Lani's body changed; she was no longer a crawling water bug but had transformed into a beautiful dragonfly.

Her wings shimmered in the sunlight, and she soared through the air with the freedom she had never imagined. The world was vast, filled with color and light she had never known existed.

In her joy, Lani remembered her promise to the friends she left behind. She tried to fly back down to the water, but her wings prevented her from returning whenever she approached the surface. She realized that she could not return to the world beneath the water.

All she could do was live fully in her new life above the pond. Lani soared higher, understanding now that her transformation was part of something greater—a journey of new life and beauty that she could not have known in her old form.

Even though she couldn't return to tell her friends, she trusted that when their time came, they, too, would understand the mystery of this transformation. Even the smallest creatures the great Creator has made can be an example to teach lessons to the seeking heart.

Consider the dragonfly, with its delicate wings and swift flight. Despite its brief existence, it fulfills its purpose. The Divine Creator is evident in all His unbelievable and small creations. In seeing the dragonfly, one may learn lessons on perseverance and adaptability. Just as the dragonfly navigates swiftly through the air, so should one be swift to obey the will of our Lord and Savior. Likewise, the dragonfly's colorful wings remind us of the beauty of accepting our exclusive design and purpose.

Dragonflies offer a great lesson on change, purpose, and focus. From their humble beginnings in the water, where they spend most of their life, to their sudden transformation into swift, lively fliers, dragonflies teach us the importance of preparation and timing. Their change reminds us of how God shapes us through extended periods of growth, often unseen until we are ready to soar into the purpose He has planned for us.

Dragonflies also show clarity of vision. Their complex eyes, with 360-degree vision, allow them to see the world with an intense focus. Likewise, in our spiritual journey, God calls us to see beyond the world's interruptions and focus on His will, seeking precision through His Word and wisdom. Just as a dragonfly accurately watches in on its prey, we are encouraged to keep our eyes on the goal, not interrupted by life's challenges.

Dragonfly's brief but excellent adult life reminds us to live fully in the present, embracing each moment with purpose. Its delicate wings and graceful movements resemble life's passing nature, urging us to trust in God's plan and make the most of the time we have been given. This way, the dragonfly teaches us to live with purpose and conversion and focus on God's greater design.

Ecclesiastes 9:10

Whatever your hand finds to do, do it with your might; for there is no work or device or knowledge or wisdom in the grave where you are going.

God wants us to know that life is precious and that each moment should be spent as if it were the last. How often have we heard someone say, "I wish I had known"? That is why there is no room for us to become irritated; it will only cause regret that cannot be destroyed and a moment lost that could have expressed love that would last as a great memory.

The dragonfly represents change and transformation. It also represents wisdom, lightness of existence or joy, flexibility, an offer to explore feelings, and being on guard against effects and deceit. Just as so many who have found Christ have climbed to a height they never dreamed of, the new Christian finds themselves in a world that they have never seen because it has always been covered by sin.

Colossians 3:23

And whatever you do, do it heartily, as to the Lord and not to men.

Dragonflies are frightening if you are a gnat, mosquito, or other minor bug. They do not simply chase down their prey; they snag them from the air with a determined aerial surprise attack. Dragonflies can judge the speed and route of a prey target and adjust their flight to capture prey.

How well do we acknowledge how close the enemy is to bringing us down? Only through God's Word will we learn of the devil's tricks. The dragonfly's exceptional, calculated aerial abilities came with their new birth. We, as Christians, go through our new birth with the indwelling of the Holy Spirit, which comes with salvation.

Dragonflies can fly in any direction, sideways and backward, and hover in a single spot for a minute or more. This exceptional ability is one characteristic of their success as they surprise attack predators; they can move in on unexpected prey from any direction.

Dragonflies help humans by controlling populations of pest insects, especially those that threaten us most, such as mosquitoes and biting flies. It has been said that a single dragonfly can eat at least thirty mosquitoes daily.

Something so small can achieve so much; they do what they were created to do. If humanity would accept their reasoning for creation, it would be a different world. God's will over humanity is to allow us to love and honor Him.

Sin and evil are, unfortunately, needed to show the opposite: our love for God and His love for us. Adam and Eve never understood the concept of love before they fell into sin. Free will does not exist if there are no good versus bad choices. In Heaven, we will be without sin.

The dragonfly only does what it was created to do; they do not try to accomplish anything else. They live the life that God intended and planned for them to do. That is all God expects of humanity: to live according to His path, not our desires. Once again, if we have questions about His will, we can turn to God's Word Inspired by the Holy Spirit.

2 Timothy 3:16–4:5

All Scripture is given by inspiration of God, and is profitable for doctrine, for reproof, for correction, for instruction in right-eousness, that the man of God may be complete, thoroughly equipped for every good work.

For centuries, dragonflies have been a symbol of inspiration and transformation. Many cultures see them as images of change and new beginnings. Art, literature, and legends often illustrate them as representations of freedom, alertness, and grace.

In many spiritual traditions, the dragonfly implies spiritual growth and explanation. Its ability to move quickly and grace-fully through the air suggests the soul's journey toward descrip-tion. Dragonflies are fascinating creatures that have given human visions for centuries.

Dragonflies' balance and coordination are also important aspects of their presence. Their tiny bodies and gentle wings give them a sense of composure and style, while their dynamic colors and complex configurations create harmony and balance.

The dragonfly's balance and harmony imply inner peace. They remind us to stay centered and balanced, even in confusion and doubt. The dragonfly's colors and patterns also represent creativity, self, and evidence, aiding us to accept and share our exceptional values with the world.

Christians should display a life of light from our inner souls filled with God's Spirit. Like the dragonfly, we cannot hide the beauty that shows God's love. As a light to the world, we reduce darkness from the lives we encounter. Christians are told to let their light shine. If we keep away from others, then our lights are hidden. The world is filled with darkness; God's children must light it up with the love of our Lord and Savior.

Matthew 5:14–16

> *You are the light of the world. A city that is set on a hill cannot be hidden. Nor do they light a lamp and put it under a basket, but on a lampstand, and it gives light to all who are in the house. Let your light so shine before men, that they may see your good works and glorify your Father in heaven.*

By strengthening our relationship with God, we will increase our light to a place high enough that the world will see it. Once it is noticed, people will want to know why you are so full of joy. Of course, the answer is easy. The love of God has taken over my life, and I know He will never leave or forsake me.

The "suppertime" call rang out, and Nathan and Grandpa took their places at the table. Grandma's homemade bread and other goodies met Nathan's bright eyes as he folded his hands and waited ... and waited. Though Grandpa was hungry too, he was adjusting his knife, fork, and plate as he finished a little conversation with Grandma.

The wait was too long for hungry Nathan, so he put his little hand on Grandpa's arm and said, "Say grace, Grampy, say grace." So, with their heads bowed, Grandpa thanked God for His love in giving Jesus to die on the cross and for the food that He had again provided for them, in the name of the Lord Jesus Christ.

Grandpa's prayer had especially pleased Nathan, so when eyes opened, he looked up at his grandpa with a satisfied smile and said, "The Lord Jesus *loves* that!"

What a truth and lesson we have from a three-year-old. The Lord does love to hear our thankfulness for everything He has provided for us. Salvation from our sins through His precious blood is, of course, the greatest. But our food, health and safety are also included in His daily care for us.[1]

The dragonfly has forgotten how it once lived deep in the water. It knows now that it is flying above the old way of life and enjoying the new life. Why would the dragonfly want to go back, or why would a Christian desire to return to the old life? It does not make sense when considering both sides of the equation.

The first thing a Christian should do is to ask God what He wants you to do or where He wants you to be. Then it would help if you learned how to stay on course, obeying and walking in the light of what has been shown to you, with complete commitment towards God.

Focus is to direct one's attention or concentrate on something. If we are focused on Christ, He becomes our thought; He and His word teach us in ways that supply our minds. Such a focus only fits because Jesus is the head of the body.

Staying on the Christian path involves spiritual practices, community involvement, and personal growth. Here are some

1. Claude Brown, *Manchild in the Promised Land*, New York: Macmillan, 1965.

critical steps to help you stay true to your faith: Take the time each day for prayer. Consistently reading and studying the Bible helps strengthen your Christian faith.

Being part of a church community provides support, fellowship, and support. Partaking in worship services and church activities can help you stay connected to your faith. Put your faith into action by helping others and volunteering for church projects or community service activities.

Accept the values of forgiveness, both for yourself and others. Holding on to bitterness can lead to a spiritual lack of progress; trying to forgive can help you grow closer to God. Surround yourself with positivity that maintains your beliefs. Jesus went to the Cross to show God's grace; we should share this love with others.

Regularly take time to improve your spiritual journey. Ask yourself how you are growing in your faith and what areas need improvement. This self-reflection can help you stay connected with your values. Combining these practices into your life can strengthen your commitment to the Christian faith and help you navigate challenges with faith and resilience.

Remembering that the dragonfly sheds its water life in the beginning and soars into the sky, we are reminded of the beautiful transformation God promises to all who trust Him. Just as the dragonfly leaves the water behind to embrace a new life of freedom and light, we, too, are called to rise above the earthly struggles and begin embracing the newness of life that God offers.

Once bound by the waters, this magnificent creature now dances in the sunlight, perfectly reflecting how we can go beyond our past and find grace, purpose, and hope through faith. In the same way, as we allow God to transform us, we, like the dragonfly, are made into something far more beautiful and accessible than we could ever imagine.

1 John 4:9

In this the love of God was manifested toward us, that God has sent His only begotten Son into the world, that we might live through Him.

Once living in sin, we were lost and without hope. Then Jesus reached down, picked us up, and cleansed us of our sins. This transition brought a new path to our lives. We can now walk joyfully, knowing this new life is much better. Like the dragonfly who lived in the water and was changed into something that could fly, we, too, have changed into something that has found the love of God.

When you live a sinful life, you don't even know that there is something better out there. The dragonfly, when it was in the dark water, probably never thought of a better life. Just like the dragonfly, we, too, weren't aware of the awesome life God had waiting for us. Through the precious blood of Christ, we can be washed clean of our sins.

Salvation is a gift, and I am so glad that God made it possible for someone like me to be saved from my sins. Now, I can fly above all that used to hold me captive. I now have something to look forward to each day.

Chapter 11

The Busy Squirrel

There was once a little squirrel who lived in a vast forest. As the leaves began to turn golden and the air grew crisp, the squirrel knew that winter was coming. Day after day, he busily gathered acorns, storing them in the hollow of an old oak tree.

His fellow forest creatures often teased him for working hard while the weather was still warm. "Why not relax and enjoy the sunshine?" they would say. But the squirrel knew that seasons would change, and the cold winds would soon blow. He continued his work, trusting that his storage would sustain him through the harsh winter.

When the snow came, the other animals scrambled for food, unprepared for the long, frozen months. But the little squirrel was safe and warm in his nest, nourished by the acorns he had carefully saved. The squirrel didn't worry when others laughed at him or doubted his preparations.

He trusted in the way the Creator had designed the world, knowing that the time to gather and rest was part of God's plan. The lesson here is that, like the squirrel, we must diligently prepare for the future, both spiritually and physically, trusting in God's wisdom and timing. Just as the squirrel stores acorns for the winter, we store up spiritual strength by staying connected to God and His Word.

Squirrels display community spirit and are known for working hard and saving for the future. Squirrels exhibit qualities that are essential for long-term survival. If humanity would stop and realize the answers are right in front of them, nature. Christians should understand that remembering God's Word will keep us on the right path.

Squirrels remember where they hide their acorns; a child of God should have His Word hidden in their hearts. Then, the Word will enable them to fulfill the task when they need it. But the knowledge we need won't be there if we don't study the Bible. We must fill our hearts and minds with His Word.

2 Timothy 3:16-17

All Scripture is given by inspiration of God, and is profitable for doctrine, for reproof, for correction, for instruction in righteousness, that the man of God may be complete, thoroughly equipped for every good work.

Studying the Bible does not have to be frightening or hard to understand as you try to start reading. Look for ways that you find interesting. You may want to begin to study the Bible book by book, verse by verse, or topic by topic; each starting point offers powerful understandings that will help you develop a daily Bible study.

Paul underwent an exciting transformation and became one of the most dedicated apostles of Christ. His life after conversion was filled with difficulties. He was imprisoned, beaten, and stoned, and even yet, through all of this, Paul remained committed to his mission to spread the gospel. He endured trials with the strength God gave him, never losing hope in the promises of Christ. He believed that the trials he experienced were temporary compared to the eternal reward he would receive in heaven. This story teaches that true persistence is embedded in faith. Christians are called to overcome hardships not by their strength but by relying on the strength and grace of God.

As Christians, we can learn several valuable lessons from Paul's endurance: Trust in God's strength, not our own. Paul's life shows that our strength to endure doesn't come from within ourselves but from God. Despite our physical and emotional struggles, we, too, can endure trials by depending on God's grace rather than relying solely on our abilities.

Keep focused on the eternal goal. Paul's unwavering focus on his heavenly reward motivated him to endure. He said in Philippians 3:14, "I press on toward the goal to win the prize for which God has called me heavenward in Christ Jesus." As Christians, we can learn to focus on our eternal destination, keeping our eyes fixed on the promises of God rather than being discouraged by temporary hardships.

Endurance leads to spiritual growth. Through suffering, we can grow in faith, patience, and character. Paul's hardships refined his dependence on God. We also glory in our sufferings because suffering produces perseverance, character, and hope. Likewise, when we face trials, they become opportunities for spiritual growth, shaping us more into Christ's image.

Encouragement to others. Paul's testimony is an encouragement to believers even today. By enduring hardship with faith, we can inspire others to keep going, showing them that God's grace is sufficient for every situation.

Perseverance in our mission, like Paul, who never hesitated from his mission despite great resistance, we should remain steadfast in what God has called us to do. Whether sharing the gospel, helping others, or growing in our faith, persistence helps us stay faithful to our purpose.

The squirrel knows that the food it stores will be needed at some point. The Christian should know that God's Word will be required at some point against the enemy or to lead a lost soul to Christ. We are told in the Bible that Jesus fought Satan with the words that are in the Holy Bible and won. That is a reminder that we, as children of God, the devil will try to turn us back into sin, so have that Word rooted deep in your heart. So, let's open the Bible up and start reading, setting an example that others can follow.

Hebrews 4:12

For the word of God is living and powerful, and sharper than any two-edged sword, piercing even to the division of soul and spirit, and of joints and marrow, and is a discerner of the thoughts and intents of the heart.

Squirrels eat a great many things that help the environment of a forest. For example, squirrels eat bark, plants, insects, caterpillars, nuts, leaves, roots and seeds. Along with all of that, they help replant the forest as they dig holes to hide their seeds/nuts. Sometimes, they don't use all the acorns. They hide and leave them, and they become trees.

Squirrels are found almost all over the world and in various climates. You can see squirrels in city parks, forests, rural communities, tropical rainforests, and some African desert areas, place; squirrels of all kinds have been able to adapt and thrive.

1 Thessalonians 5:18

In everything, give thanks; for this is the will of God in Christ Jesus for you.

Our lives can be an example, like when we see a squirrel jumping enthusiastically. We stop to view the moment, as others will stop to find out what has put that smile on your face. Salvation through Christ changes our attitude. We look at our surroundings through the window of love.

As the squirrel plans, we should learn to plan our lives to serve God. We don't know what tomorrow will bring; if you are a born-again Christian, it could be the day the Lord calls you home. The Bible speaks about His return; it could be any day now. The squirrel teaches us that hard work pays off; they are always ready for winter.

Matthew 24:42–44

Watch, therefore, for you do not know what hour your Lord is coming. But know this, that if the master of the house had known what hour the thief would come, he would have watched and not allowed his house to be broken into. Therefore, you also be ready, for the Son of Man is coming at an hour you do not expect."

The squirrel is ready. He has been preparing for the time when he won't be able to find any food. We should prepare for the Lord's return by seeking His will through prayer and reading His Word. We should seek the lost so they will also be ready. I believe it is time for God's children to get busy. Time is being wasted, and souls are dying lost.

1 John 3: 2–3

> *Beloved, now we are children of God, and it has not yet been revealed what we shall be, but we know that when He is revealed, we shall be like Him, for we shall see Him as He is. And everyone who has this hope in Him purifies himself, just as He is pure.*

Jesus is coming again—personally and visibly. He will return to complete His redeeming mission and eternal kingdom in power and glory. Some Christians may disagree on details surrounding the end times, but we can agree that Jesus is coming again.

Just as the squirrels know winter is just around the corner, they spend most of their time preparing for it. We could learn from them. Christians should realize that the Lord could come today. Are you ready? With our steadfast focus on the Lord Jesus Christ, everything else will fall into place.

1 Thessalonians 4:16–17

> *For the Lord Himself will descend from heaven with a shout, with the voice of an archangel, and with the trumpet of God. And the dead in Christ will rise first. Then we who are alive and remain shall be caught up together with them in the clouds to meet the Lord in the air. And thus, we shall always be with the Lord.*

Have you ever noticed that squirrels are always chewing on something? There is a reason for the continual chewing their front teeth would grow into their lower jaw. A lesson can be learned: if we continue to delete the sin in our lives, we will not fall away from the Lord. Just as the squirrel knows, there would be a problem if they stopped working on keeping their teeth smaller.

Squirrels sometimes rub an acorn on their face, increasing their chances of finding it when needed. The word of God must fill our hearts with an understanding of God's perfect will through Jesus Christ. Christians need to know how to live in a world of corruption and show them the joy of the Lord.

They are always watching for predators that could end their lives, and we should be aware of our surroundings because we know that the enemy wants to turn us around. The devil would like for the child of God to fall into as much sin as he throws at them. We have many backups for things that can go wrong in our lives, and our spiritual life needs to be reminded that the Lord is here for us even in difficult times. Trust in Him and know you are surrounded by God's love, which will see you through any obstacle.

Deuteronomy 31:6

Be strong and of good courage, do not fear nor be afraid of them; for the Lord your God, He is the One who goes with you. He will not leave you nor forsake you.

This small animal seems fearless at times; it will start calling at even a person coming too close to its territory. As Christians, we should know that when we are tempted, we should call out in the name of Jesus for escape from the substance. Fighting with the Word of God will bring us victory. To be ready for that situation, we will need to continue in our daily study of the Bible.

Proverbs 4:16–27

For they do not sleep unless they have done evil; And their sleep is taken away unless they make someone fall. For they eat the bread of wickedness And drink the wine of violence. But the path of the just is like the shining sun That shines ever brighter unto the perfect day. The way of the wicked is like darkness; They do not know what makes them stumble. My son, give attention to my words; Incline your ear to my sayings. Do not let them depart from your eyes; Keep them in the midst of your heart; For they are life to those who find them And health to all their flesh. Keep your heart with all diligence, For out of it spring the issues of life. Put away from you a deceitful mouth And put perverse lips far from you. Let your eyes look straight ahead, And your eyelids look right before you. Ponder the path of your feet. And let all your ways be established. Do not turn to the right or the left; Remove your foot from evil.

Chapter 12

The Loving Hen

S omewhere on the prairie, a young man decided to build a small farm. He worked hard first, then built a house—not big, but comfortable. The next was a small barn for the animals he would eventually get.

Just before he bought some animals, he built a fence in front of the barn to keep the animals under control when they were outside. After that, he was ready to go to town and buy some farm animals.

First, he bought a horse and donkey, then a hen with small chicks. He was proud of his success because everything was falling into place. Now it was time to plant a garden; using the donkey to plow and lay the rows for planting, his garden was ready.

The mother hen, with her young chicks, could roam free. The farmer loved watching how the hen would lead the chicks around the field, especially the chick always wandering off. The mother hen would go to crowing loudly. The little chick would run back in line as soon as she did. The farmer would watch this as often as he could.

One day, the farmer saw a cloud of smoke not far from his property. Knowing it was getting closer, he released his animals from the barn. There was a large creek near the barn, so he and the animals went across the creek to safety.

After the fire had gone out, the farmer realized his house, fence, and barn were gone. As he walked around angrily, he noticed a burnt lump. He went up and kicked it. As soon as he did, all the little chicks came out; the mother hen stayed with her young to put her wings around them and protect them from the fire.

If you pay close attention, you will notice that during the 21 days of trying to hatch her eggs, she loses weight due to restricted movement, which leads to reduced feeding. She's sacrificed this much because of her desire to hatch the eggs with the result, her little chicks. As the mother hen sits on her eggs for those 21 days with maximum intensity. Her primary aim and objective usually are to hatch the eggs.

A mother hen can be seen as a powerful illustration of godly principles, mainly reflecting themes of protection, care, and sacrificial love. In nature, a mother hen shows attributes that can display spiritual truths. Just as a hen spreads her wings to protect her chicks from danger, the Bible teaches us that God offers refuge to His children.

God's sacrificial love and protection for His children. Just as the hen does not abandon her chicks in their time of need, neither does God leave us when we face problems. He is our continuous guard, willing to shelter us at any cost, even sacrificing Himself to keep us safe.

Proverbs 16:3

Commit your works to the Lord, And your thoughts will be established.

The mother hen provides warmth, protection, and guidance, teaching her chicks where to find food and how to avoid danger. This is how God guides and cares for us spiritually, always protecting and leading us according to His will, even when we may not fully understand the danger around us. This similarity can show trust, security, and how God's love includes all aspects of our lives, just as the mother hen's love covers her helpless chicks.

The selfless nature of a mother's sacrificial love shows us the ultimate sacrifice made by Jesus Christ on the cross for the redemption of our sins. Mother hens illustrate this sacrificial love in their daily care for their chicks. Let us honor the mother hens for their earthly role and as reflections of God's character and love for His children.

Romans 15:13

Now may the God of hope fill you with all joy and peace in believing that you may abound in hope by the power of the Holy Spirit.

God will never leave you if you make Him your resting place. Nothing will separate you from this God because His power works, and His purpose is to be with you always. Even if the worst somehow comes, He knows what it will take to bring you out of destruction into a joyful state of mind. Knowing that you need God's assistance will bring you to Him every time, just like the chicks run to the mother hen.

A hen raises her chicks, offering warmth and reassurance. This represents the reassuring existence of God, who promises never to leave nor forsake His children. The hen's behavior also illustrates how God nurtures, protects, and guides His children.

In the same way, God's protection is being safe from harm under the shelter of His wings. Just as the chicks trust and follow their mother's lead, we are called to trust in the guidance and protection of our Lord and Savior, knowing that He guards us carefully.

The chick's trust in their mother strongly compares faith and confidence in God. Just as chicks automatically trust their mother hen to protect, nurture, and guide them, we are called to trust God's care and guidance.

Proverbs 3:5–6

Trust in the Lord with all your heart And lean not on your own understanding; In all your ways acknowledge Him, And He shall direct your paths.

A mother hen cares for her chicks in several basic ways. After hatching, she sits on them to keep them warm, especially during chilly weather. Chickens cannot regulate their body temperature well when young, so the hen's body heat is necessary for survival.

Chicks rest peacefully under their mother's care because they know they are safe. In the same way, our faith in God's love allows us to find peace, knowing He watches over us with enduring care. The mother hen instinctively protects her chicks from possible threats.

She will cluck softly to call them and can display forceful behaviors toward predators. This protective behavior helps keep her chicks safe from larger animals. A hen also teaches her chicks how to find food.

She scratches at the ground to uncover seeds, insects, and other edible items, encouraging her chicks to copy her movements and learn to search for themselves. The mother hen teaches her chicks about their social structure through different calls and behaviors needed to develop within the flock.

The hen helps clean her chicks by gently picking at them,

providing comfort and bonding. A mother hen is attentive and nurturing, ensuring her chicks grow strong and healthy as they begin their lives. Chicks' obedience to the hen can represent spiritual lessons.

The obedience of chicks following their mother can characterize the call for believers to obey God's guidance and direction. Just as the chicks instinctively trust and follow their mother without question, we should follow God's Word.

Just as the chicks' obedience to the mother hen keeps them safe from predators and harm, our obedience to God's commands protects us from spiritual threats and leads to peace and security. The chicks obey the hen not out of fear but of faith in her ability to care for them. This can mirror the faithful obedience believers are called to have towards God's authority, trusting that His guidance is always for our good.

The mother hen's wings not only protect When her chicks cry out to her for help, but she calls them to "come quick and hide." When she foresees danger and strife. As well as keeping her baby chicks safe, she is ready to fight off enemy attacks. She cherishes them and keeps them warm from the bleak winter cold and storms.

God's gracious love we can compare to the mother hen's love for her chicks, so dear God protects and cherishes His beloved under His Almighty wings of love.

God's wings of love are not weak like feathers but as strong as bulletproof steel armor. Yet as flexible, warm, and soft as feathers to completely encompass and comfort us. When you feel afraid or feel like easy prey, God invites us to run to Him. History shows how He protects people who trust and have faith in Him.[1]

---

1. Beverley Joy @ 2014 Simply Story Poetry.

Psalm 91:1–2

*He who dwells in the secret place of the Most High Shall abide
under the shadow of the Almighty. I will say of the Lord, "He
is my refuge and my fortress; My God, in Him I will trust.*

Our faith in God will lead us to the comfort of His love; our
God is our refuge. Grab the love God has planted in your heart
when nothing seems right. Then, you can rest in peace through
His mighty power.

Psalm 62:7

*In God is my salvation and my glory; The rock of my strength,
And my refuge is in God.*

We are in the way both of duty and comfort when our souls
wait upon God; when we cheerfully give up ourselves and all
our affairs to His will and wisdom; when we leave ourselves
to all the ways of His providence and patiently expect the
event, with satisfaction in His goodness. See the ground and
reason for this dependence. By His grace, He has supported
me, and by His providence, He has delivered me.

He can only be my Rock and my salvation; creatures are
nothing without Him, and I will look above them to Him.
Trusting in God, the heart is fixed. If God be for us, we need
not fear what man can do against us. Having put his confidence in God, David foresees his enemies' overthrow. We
have found it good to wait upon the Lord and should charge
our souls to have such constant dependence upon Him, as
may make us always easy.

If God will save my soul, I may leave everything else to
His disposal, knowing all shall turn to my salvation. And as
David's faith in God advances to an unshaken steadfastness,

his joy in God improves into a holy triumph. Meditation and prayer are blessed means of strengthening faith and hope.

Realizing God's love and mighty power is the beginning of a born-again Christian's life. As we grow, our trust in Him grows with us. Watching the chicks follow their mother hen is an excellent lesson on dependence. The chicks don't look for anyone else to follow, even when they wander away to explore their world. When in doubt, they run to the mother hen.

Sometimes, in our walk with Jesus, we wander away from all the attractions in our world. Some forget that the Lord is still there to comfort them. At that time, the fall can be fatal; unless we reach out to Him, the situation will only get worse. This is not an option.

Jesus is waiting for you to seek Him, ready to save you from destruction.

Some people seem inclined to make bad decisions, and you may be one of them. Maybe your emotions get in the way and overwhelm you, and instead of stopping to think through the decision, you follow your feelings and act unwisely. Or perhaps you let other people influence you wrongly, and you end up following their advice.

The lesson from those little chicks is not to turn to something else because the hen was all they needed or wanted. Christians should know that Christ is all that we need. He is with us during good times and is there when there seems to be no hope. The Lord is our hope; with our faith in Him, life will work out.

If you have ever watched those little chicks, you know how curious they are. They are bad at wandering off to investigate their surroundings and then get into trouble. If not from their adventure, it sometimes comes from the mother hen.

It is amazing how well the chicks listen to the mother hen;

they never question her. Children of God should listen to the guidance of the Holy Spirit through our hearts and in God's Word. The mother hen's only concern is the care of her chicks. The Lord is concerned about all His creations. Yet, humanity has been offered the gift of salvation by grace through faith.

Jeremiah 23:24

"Can anyone hide himself in secret places, So I shall not see him?" says the LORD; "Do I not fill heaven and earth?" says the LORD.

Our God is watching over us; we need not worry, for He is all-powerful and strong. Trust in Him as the chicks trust the mother hen: no questions asked, do what she says. So, we should listen to God.

As we have seen, a mother hen protects their chicks; she will tell them to hide if she is away. If she is close enough, the hen will put them under her wings no matter the risk of her life. Sometimes, the hen will move away from her chicks to distract the predators.

Isaiah 53:5

But He was wounded for our transgressions, He was bruised for our iniquities; The chastisement for our peace was upon Him, And by His stripes we are healed.

God sent His only begotten Son to suffer and die to wash away our sins. Without the blood He shed on the cross, we would be lost and without hope. By grace, we are saved through faith, which means that even though we did not see Him go through all He did for us, we accept and believe that this did happen. Each person who receives and follows the path of salvation by faith can feel the indwelling of the Holy Spirit at their new birth—reassuring us of our new beginning.

Chapter 13

The World of the Deer

In a peaceful forest, a young deer roamed gracefully, always alert to the dangers of the wild. As dawn broke, the deer ventured to a clear stream for a drink one morning. The forest was calm, but the deer's senses were sharp, its ears attuned to the slightest rustle of leaves. Suddenly, a strong wind stirred, and the animals in the forest scattered, sensing an approaching storm.

But the deer stood firm, eyes wide and ears flicking. It did not run at the first sign of trouble, for it trusted in its instincts and ability to find shelter when needed. Quietly, it moved toward the densest part of the forest, where the thick trees would offer protection.

As the storm raged outside, the deer rested beneath the trees, unharmed, waiting for the skies to clear. While other creatures panicked, the deer's calmness allowed it to find safety. The storm passed, and the deer emerged into the sunlit forest, ready to continue its journey.

Psalm 42: 1–2

> *As the deer pants for the water brooks, So pants my soul for*
> *You, O God. My soul thirsts for God, for the living God. When*
> *shall I come and appear before God?*

Remaining calm and steadfast in the face of difficulties, knowing God will provide strength to bear and overcome. Like the deer seeking shelter beneath the trees, we should realize that God is our greatest security and shield during life's storms. The deer's calmness can be seen as evidence of the peace God gives to those who trust in Him and remain steadfast during tough times

Deer are most active in the early morning and late evening. Though to a lesser degree, they are also active at night. Being an animal of the twilight implies that deer are most active at night and during times of low light. Deer have exceptional vision and hearing, which offers them a reasonable edge over predators at these times.

Around May or June, the forest is graced with the arrival of new life. Guided by nature's wisdom, the doe gives birth to one or two fawns. Hidden in a secluded shelter, these newborns make a speckled entrance into the world. Extremely well-fully developed, they stand and walk within minutes, their spotted fur acting as a beautiful coat of camouflage, shielding them from the eyes of predators as they begin their amazing journey of life.

As the doe supports parental care, she nurtures her fawns for several months. Nature's splendid beauty is revealed as she provides critical nutrients. In this gentle moment, she teaches necessary skills and survival tactics, producing a bond that bonds protection and independence.

In the Bible, the deer is often used to symbolize grace, swiftness, and beauty. It is also associated with seeking God and finding refuge in Him, representing the soul's longing for God. The deer's ability to navigate difficult landscapes and its intelligent sense of direction are qualities Christians should strive to follow in their spiritual journey.

Psalm 18:33–36

He makes my feet like the feet of deer And sets me on my high places. He teaches my hands to make war, So that my arms can bend a bow of bronze. You have also given me the shield of Your salvation; Your right hand has held me up. Your gentleness has made me great. You enlarged my path under me, So my feet did not slip.

Deer are often connected with grace and swiftness. These animals are known for their ability to move swiftly and gracefully through the forest, suggesting the importance of being quick in our lives. Just as a deer can easily navigate obstacles, we are often connected to God's grace, swiftness, and quickness.

Deer are also known for their keen sense of awareness and alertness. In the Bible, deer are often used to symbolize watchfulness and focus. Just as a deer is always looking for danger, we, too, can learn to be alert and aware of our surroundings. This can help us stay alert to potential threats and make wise decisions. We know that just as the deer are hunted, so the Christians are sought by Satan. This devil is always striving to find a way to end us permanently.

1 Peter 5:8

Be sober, be vigilant; because your adversary the devil walks about like a roaring lion, seeking whom he may devour.

Christians should read the Bible for inspiration and guidance on life's journey. The Bible contains descriptions that help us better understand the spiritual world around us. The deer is one of the animals in the Bible that indicates we should learn from them.

Just as there is a season to hunt deer, it is always an open season for humanity. The enemy of your hope and happiness hunts with that same instinct. Satan prowls like a roaring lion, seeking someone to overcome. And because he's cunning, he spends much of his time among and suffering. He lies in wait, wanting to exhaust the volatile and helpless.

Everything that might tempt us to doubt God and His goodness is meant to lead us to Him and prove that He's engaged in a massive spiritual battle for our lives.

A powerful, forceful, and creative enemy wants to kill you. God's unlimited resources and power will meet and offer to us for His suffering people. With God's persistent compassion and attention when they gather around and put their trust in God's Word.

Most deer run away when they see humans due to their instinct to avoid predators. Deer are target animals and have evolved to be highly alert to probable threats. Their responsive senses of sight, hearing, and smell help them identify danger. When deer notice a threat, their instant reaction is to flee. The deer is a social animal; if one deer senses danger and runs, others in the group will likely follow, supporting the behavior. Their swift reaction is a detailed survival strategy.

The Bible teaches us about sin and how God wants everyone to escape it. God's warnings, like the fire alarm, are for our good and protection. We don't always want to hear what God says. There are some reasons we might choose to ignore God's warning. We might be set on our plan. We think that the situation will turn out well. In our understanding, we can't see how anything wrong could result from the situation.

Ephesians 6:10

Finally, my brethren, be strong in the Lord and in the power of His might.

We run with God to higher spiritual places by accepting His Word as accurate even when we don't feel like it. He leads us to run with Him by, making our feet like the feet of a deer, aiding us to stand on the heights, to stand on His promises without falling. We can stand with confidence and competence, responsiveness, and stability. The following two verses represent the spiritual symbols of our lives.

Habakkuk 3:19

The Lord God is my strength; He will make my feet like deer's feet, And He will make me walk on my high hills.

2 Samuel 22:34

He makes my feet like the feet of deer And sets me on my high places.

We are not to separate from God after our brief morning connections. After our quiet time, Bible reading, and prayers, we must stay connected with our Lord Jesus. Since Jesus lives within us, we should be aware of His presence. We ought to hear His whisper, speak to Him, and see our situation from His perspective.

Have you ever spent time with someone so excited about football that it seemed that was all they talked about? How much more should a child of God enjoy and share their love for the new life He has given to those who have accepted Christ?

Every believer experiences seasons constantly with their faith journeys, like those in the natural world: stormy seasons, seasons of fresh growth, and long, hot, dry seasons. Your faith will survive and increase in the mountains and valleys, but you'll need to drink from the Living Water our Savior has provided.

As they develop from birth to adulthood, fawns learn many things from their mothers, including how to survive and interact with other deer. They learn to listen to their mother's vocal commands and nose nudges, lay down, and stay still when told to.

In their early years, fawns learn to hide from predators by lying still and using their camouflage and low scent to blend in. If we listen, God will reach out spiritually to keep us from falling by the wayside. All we must do is listen, just like the fawns listen to their mother; no question asked; they do what they are told.

We must decide that obedience is a priority and make it a part of our lives. Trust God: Trust that God's way is best for you and that He will provide for your needs. Follow God's word, reflect on it, and act on it. Put others before yourself and be gracious.

It is important to focus on the fact that God is always with us. Obeying God can be a joy and a way to grow one's faith and get closer to him. James said in his written word that we should draw closer to God, and then God will draw closer. God will never choose for you and has given us free will.

James 4:8

Draw near to God and He will draw near to you. Cleanse your hands, you sinners, and purify your hearts, you double-minded.

So many things can go wrong when we live based on feelings rather than truth. Feelings are unstable, occasionally disloyal, and often foolish. Feelings are a gift, but God's Spirit must control them. Our emotions, as well as our thoughts and will, can trick us.

The fawn's obedience response is likely due to instinct rather than the doe's instruction, but it can teach us. Those little fawns trust their mothers so much that they are obedient even unto death. Obedience to God is part of a Christian's connection with God and can be shown in many ways.

1 Corinthians 15:58

Therefore, my beloved brethren, be steadfast, immovable, always abounding in the work of the Lord, knowing that your labor is not in vain in the Lord.

When we became God's children, He filled us with the Holy Spirit to guide and comfort us; we then felt God's presence. He speaks to our hearts to better understand our path in this life. The Bible teaches that we should not quench the Holy Spirit. If we do this, He will not be able to help us; we must listen to Him.

1 John 5: 1–5

Whoever believes that Jesus is the Christ is born of God, and everyone who loves Him who begot also loves him who is begotten of Him. By this we know that we love the children of God, when we love God and keep His commandments. For this is the love of God, that we keep His commandments. And His commandments are not burdensome. For whatever is born of God overcomes the world. And this is the victory that has overcome the world—our faith. Who is he who overcomes the world, but he who believes that Jesus is the Son of God?

In the book of Romans, Paul tells us that life is full of struggles; he even gives examples of how sin tries to take over your life. The fawns would undoubtedly like to explore their world, but only what their mother allows. As children of God, we should only do the things that please Him. Some might respond by saying, "How can I know?" His Word is like a road map to lead us in the right direction and keep us on course.

Romans 7: 8–12

But sin, taking opportunity by the commandment, produced in me all manner of evil desire. For apart from the law sin was dead. I was alive once without the law, but when the commandment came, sin revived, and I died. And the commandment, which was to bring life, I found to bring death. For sin, taking occasion by the commandment, deceived me, and by it killed me. Therefore, the law is holy, and the commandment holy and just and good.

Chapter 14

The Wisdom of the Owl

In the quiet forest, as night fell and all other creatures retreated to rest, the owl remained still and watchful, waiting. It did not rush or flutter like the sparrows or fret like the mice. With piercing eyes, it could see what others could not, finding its way through the dark with clarity and precision.

The other animals often mocked the owl, wondering why it did not move hurriedly or engage in their daytime worries. But the owl understood that wisdom comes from patience and observation, not hasty actions. When danger loomed, or the way was unclear, the owl always knew the path to safety, guiding others with its knowledge of unseen things.

Just as the owl can see in the darkness, those who trust in God and seek His wisdom can navigate the uncertainties of life. The darkness may confuse or frighten others, but we can discern the right path with spiritual insight, relying on patience and trust in God's timing rather than acting out of fear.

In spiritual observations, owls are often linked with wisdom and knowledge. Owls have long been representations of wisdom, often due to their ability to see in darkness, supporting the idea of having insight or understanding where others cannot. This could represent the wisdom that comes from God. Owls' sharp vision in the night implies the ability to discern truth and deception, even under challenging conditions.

Proverbs 2:6

> *For the LORD gives wisdom; From His mouth come knowledge and understanding.*

The owl can represent waiting on God's timing and trusting in His plan. It is often seen as an indication of having a broad perspective or the ability to see things others cannot, the more profound truth that only faith can reveal.

Owls are of the night, associated with the night and the unknown. Spiritually, this can indicate our journey through dark times or the unknown, where we can trust in God's invisible guidance even in times of doubt or difficulty.

The night is as bright as the day because we walk in light with Christ. The owl's spiritual values highlight God-given wisdom, the importance of discernment, and how spiritual insight guides believers through life's darkness.

> Seeing or hearing an owl might serve as a reminder of God's diverse and wondrous creation. In the Book of Job, we are reminded that God's wisdom is displayed in the instincts and abilities He has given to animals (Job 39). The owl, with its remarkable adaptations for nocturnal life, can inspire us to marvel at the Creator's ingenuity and care for all creatures, even those that operate in the darkness.[1]

---

1. *ChristianPure.* (2024, August 30th). Retrieved from biblical mysteries of the owl: https://christianpure.com/learn/what-does-an-owl-symbolizein-the-bible/

For some Christians, an encounter with an owl might prompt reflection on the theme of spiritual awakening. Just as owls are alert in the darkness, we, too, are called to be spiritually awake and vigilant, even in times of difficulty or obscurity. As Saint Paul writes in 1 Thessalonians 5:5–6:

For you are all children of light, children of the day. We are not of the night or of the darkness. So then, let us not sleep, as others do, but let us stay awake and sober.

The Bible doesn't explicitly label owls as a bad omen. Their symbolism is more nuanced and reflects spiritual realities rather than good or bad fortune. While owls are often associated with desolation and abandonment, it's important to remember that they are used as symbols, not literal predictors of future events.[2]

Psalm 139:12

Indeed, the darkness shall not hide from You, But the night shines as the day; The darkness and the light are both alike to You.

Owls are aware of their surroundings and can be alert to opportunities. They can teach us to be more mindful and live in the moment. Owls can rotate their heads 270 degrees in each direction, teaching us to consider multiple views when making choices.

Owls have keen eyesight and are competent at night, which

---

2. *ChristianPure.* (2024, August 30th). Retrieved from biblical mysteries of the owl: https://christianpure.com/learn/what-does-an-owl-symbolizein-the-bible/

can teach us about confirmation and strong awareness. Owls are associated with religion and the ability to navigate the unseen realms of knowledge.

The heart of our Father looks and reaches beyond what is seen by our natural eye and even what we know presently through discernment. He looks beyond a person's outer surface and the inner condition of their soul.

He looks beyond a person's history and sees a much-loved child of God, someone with a hopeful identity and future in His Kingdom. A word of love and evidence from God often breaks down the barriers, bondages, and hurts that a person carries. He takes great delight in showing that love to them and others through His creative ministry.

Owls are generally solitary creatures. They tend to live and hunt alone, especially outside the breeding season. However, during mating and nesting periods, they form pairs, and some species may gather in small groups, but for the most part, they are known for their independent behavior.

The solitary nature of owls can be seen as a metaphor for certain aspects of the Christian walk. Just as owls spend much of their lives alone, Christians are often called to periods of solitude or personal consideration for their spiritual journey.

Psalm 46:10

Be still and know that I am God; I will be exalted among the nations, I will be exalted in the earth!

These times of separation from the world allow believers to grow in their relationship with Christ and develop spiritual strength for the encounters ahead. Also, the owl's acute awareness and sharp senses could reflect how Christians are called to be watchful and discerning.

The owl's isolated nature is related to the Christian experience of seeking God in stillness. Christians should develop sensitivity, learning to hear God's voice within the world's noise.

Matthew 7:12

Therefore, whatever you want men to do to you, do also to them, for this is the Law and the Prophets.

Christians should associate and commit to each other because they love Christ and His people; their desire to be with other believers shows they are supporters. Giving yourself to regularly assembling with other believers is substantial evidence of true love for Christ and His people. You will gain their help and encouragement to be faithful to Christ through the trials of life, and you will be able to encourage others as well.

Hebrews 10:25

Not forsaking the assembling of ourselves together, as is the manner of some, but exhorting one another, and so much the more as you see the Day approaching.

All our individuality as members of Christ's body displays something of the nature of God when we're one and when we display this oneness to the world. The divine unity of Father, Son, and Spirit, enjoyed from before the foundation of the world, the joy and happiness that overflows that union of eternal love, is what Jesus wants for His disciples.

He wants our joy fulfilled and for us to be one, just as He and the Father are. We've been adopted into the family, united to Christ, and therefore united to God.

Christian unity matters so the world will know we're Christ's followers, but there's a more profound sense in which it shows the world what God is like. A deeper sense follows: Christian unity participates in God's divine life as Three-in-One. God's children seek to serve Him through love and obedience; the young wolves each want to please the other older wolves in their pack, and Christians want to please God.

The whole point of the church is to work to gather so that each person will be fed the proper Word of God for future guidance. New converts will be looking for examples of how to walk like Christ. The older members of the church should be the best ones. The longer we serve the Lord, the stronger we should become in His Word and our walk.

Church unity matters because our unity is connected to the unity of God Himself. Our conflicts are a disgraceful insult to the gospel. When we participate in His divine love, the world sees a reflection of God's inner life in our fellowship. It's how we withstand the pressures of the world that rage against God's truth.

The Bible tells us that pure and clean faith means, in God's eyes, caring for those who have no one else to care for them. Helping others is a natural way to share God's love. No matter how busy we are or how little we have, giving is a blessing for the giver and the one who receives it.

James 2:14–17

> *What does it profit, my brethren, if someone says he has faith but does not have works? Can faith save him? If a brother or sister is naked and destitute of daily food, and one of you says to them, "Depart in peace, be warmed and filled," but you do not give them the things which are needed for the body, what does it profit? Thus, also faith by itself, if it does not have works, is dead.*

Many feel that work for Christian unity is not especially

urgent or important in the difficulties of our modern world. So many different issues demand the attention of committed Christians, such as responding to global crises in which people are suffering, developing strong moral stands on various moral problems and challenges, etc. Such issues must remain of significant importance to Christians.

However, Christians form the one body of Christ. If that body remains divided and split, lacking unity, agreement, and harmony, the Christian witness will be completely reduced. Through the lifestyle of the wolf, I have attempted to demonstrate the importance of Christianity.

As Christians, we must hold to God's Word for direction. Though the world changes, the child of God remains steadfast. Christians have a complete map of their journey to paradise. So, there is no reason to get off course because there is only one direction to heaven.

Ask God to help you make wise decisions that will follow His will. Remember, God loves you and knows what is best for you. Why not seek His will, even in small things? When you decide, ponder and pray.

Trusting God is an essential element of true and saving faith that looks to God and finds peace, strength, contentment, and much more in him, and all that he has done, is doing, and will do, both now and forever in His Son Jesus Christ.

Everything about God is trustworthy because of who He is in the perfection of His being. The Bible elucidates this great truth in two ways: first, it warns about the folly of trusting in anyone or anything other than the Lord, and second, it describes for us His unique glory. [3]

---

3. Kirk Wellum, "Trusting God," (The Gospel Coalition, INC, 2024) thegosplecoalition.org

Philippians 4:6–7

Be anxious for nothing, but in everything by prayer and supplication, with thanksgiving, let your requests be made known to God; and the peace of God, which surpasses all understanding, will guard your hearts and minds through Christ Jesus.

Learning to trust Christ for the things that are needed is a difficult lesson. This is because what we need is different from what we want. I have heard it said that both a millionaire and a poor man would end up six feet in the ground with nothing from this world.

The number of things you possess will not matter in the end. The main thing is whether you have accepted Jesus Christ as your Lord and Savior will decide where you will spend eternity. Today is the day of salvation; tomorrow may not come, but our decisions determine our outcome in life.

Chapter 15

The Fox

There lived a fox known for its intelligence and quick thinking. A great storm was coming one day, and all the animals were busy preparing. The fox, confident in its ability to survive anything, did nothing. It thought I am clever enough to outsmart any danger. Why waste time preparing? When the storm arrived, it was fiercer than anyone expected. The fox ran from shelter to shelter, always finding himself in danger. The animals who had prepared their homes endured the storm safely, while the fox struggled to find refuge despite all its cleverness. After the storm passed, the fox realized that wisdom is not only in cunning but in preparation and humility. It vowed never again to rely solely on its cleverness but also to heed the wisdom of the diligent and humble creatures around it.

Foxes possess several traits that can offer valuable spiritual and life lessons. They are highly adaptable animals capable of living in various environments, from forests to urban areas. This shows us the importance of adaptability in our faith and life, of being ready to face change and challenges with grace and resilience. Spiritual adaptability means trusting in God through changing circumstances and being open to new paths He may lead us on.

Foxes thrive in any environment. They aren't picky about what they eat. Their diet depends on what food is available in the area. They eat birds, vegetables, worms, fish, fruit, frogs, etc. They make the best of any situation. The fox has an extraordinary hearing ability, and it knows it. It can hear low-frequency sounds, which helps it pinpoint and target its prey. Thus, it focuses on honing that ability from pup to adulthood.

Overall, they encompass their cunning, intelligence, resourcefulness, and association with trickery and deception. These traits have made foxes fascinating creatures in various cultural contexts, capturing people's imagination and inspiring stories and legends throughout history. They have also taught us to stop and think about being more watchful.

Foxes teach us the importance of being flexible and adaptable. They remind us that change is a natural part of life and that we should embrace it rather than resist it. These clever creatures symbolize the power of perception and quick thinking. Observing a fox teaches us to trust our instincts and make wise decisions in times of uncertainty.

God's preceptive will is His revealed will in the Bible. This is the will that God wants us to know. Everything we need to know to live in this world is written on those pages. There's no missing information we must seek out in mysterious, unknown places. It's not hidden somewhere, like in a scavenger hunt, and we just have to find it. It's all there.

The Bible teaches us what is sinful and what is not. It tells us the purpose of our life: to glorify God. It tells us how to treat others, how to steward what he has provided, how to love our family, and how to live and work and rest. Most of all, it shows us our greatest need—redemption from sin—and reveals our great Savior, whose life, death, and resurrection are sufficient to free us from sin and enable us to live in righteousness. God's Word also teaches us about the Spirit, who lives within us, producing the fruit of holiness and helping us to daily put sin to death. Ultimately, God's will for our life is that we grow in holiness, that we become more like Christ. [1]

When you think of a protector, some imagine a strong and loyal fox guarding its family and territory. Foxes have long been associated with the role of protectors in various cultures, representing the importance of family and home.

Like a fox fiercely defends its den and offspring, we can learn from their dedication and loyalty to our families. They remind us of the importance of creating a safe and nurturing environment for our loved ones.

As the fox creates a safe home for its family, Christian homes should be marked for God and reflect Jesus in everything we do. It needs to be evident that Christ is alive there. To build a godly home, we must center it around God, His will, His desires, and His Word. He should be the hub instead of just a spoke.

Our homes say a lot about us. How we spend our time there, how we decorate, and what we do inside its walls speaks volumes about what we believe. As Christians, our homes should be marked for God and reflect Jesus in everything we do.

It needs to be evident that Christ is alive there. To build a godly home, we must center it around God, His will, desires, and Word. He should be the center instead of just a simple

1. C. Fox, (2017, August 29th). *God's Wisdom and Decision Making*. Retrieved from A Heart Set Free: https://www.christinafox.com/blog/2017/8/17/gods-wisdom-anddecision-making

topic. Ideally, our houses should be places of worship rather than just structures where we eat, sleep, and play.

Foxes are curious and easily distracted, and humans are the same way. Many things compete for God's position on the throne of our hearts. In our American culture, we serve the idols of convenience, entertainment, prosperity, and self. These things get in the way of truly honoring God and receiving His blessings over our homes and families.

Do we desire to connect with Netflix more than renew our minds with Scripture? Do we favor quick fixes rather than putting in the hard work of consistently disciplining and training our children? Are we too focused on the short-term goals of financial gain instead of the things that will last for eternity?

Joshua 24:15

And if it seems evil to you to serve the Lord, choose for your-selves this day whom you will serve, whether the gods your fathers served that were on the other side of the river or the gods of the Amorites, in whose land you dwell. But for me and my house, we will serve the Lord.

If we want to live honestly, we must remove what takes the place of God's rule in our house. We must lead by example so that what we teach can be seen in our actions. Making the right choices is one of the most important lessons we can demonstrate.

Each of us will have to make many decisions. If we concentrate on putting Christ first, those decisions will come together correctly. The world has plenty of things to redirect your attention; focus on why you don't want to live like the world and focus on Christ.

Thinking about how the foxes find ways to overcome their

surroundings, somehow, they find ways to blend in without changing their identity. We might consider how we can still live in a lost world without hope that we will be able to live the life God put before us.

Yet, studying the Bible will teach us another side to those sneaky little foxes. They can get into things that others would avoid, and they are known to tear up things around them.

Foxes in the Bible symbolize cunning, craftiness, and destructiveness. They represent minor temptations or distractions that can erode faith. In biblical stories, foxes illustrate human characteristics, inspired action, and spiritual truths.

The foxes often portray negative traits and remind us of caution and faith. In Scripture, foxes include cunning, destructiveness, flexibility, and resourcefulness as warnings and lessons for spiritual wisdom and integrity. Christian tradition views foxes as symbols of temptation and sin, calling for caution, sensitivity, sound doctrine, and a balance of knowledge and innocence in our spiritual lives.

Yet, we must also remember that every creature in God's creation has its place and purpose. While foxes may symbolize negative traits in some contexts, they also remind us of God's care for all His creatures. Our Lord Jesus Himself speaks of foxes.

Foxes in the Bible symbolize the banished or outcasts. The prophet Ezekiel compares false prophets to "foxes among ruins" suggesting those who take advantage of others' misfortunes. This image calls us to examine our hearts and actions, ensuring that we do not exploit the vulnerable but instead reach out to them with Christ's love.

Ezekiel 13:4

O Israel, your prophets are like foxes in the deserts.

In all these symbolic uses, foxes in Scripture invite us to reflect on our lives, our relationship with God, and our behavior toward others. They remind us of the need for wisdom, discernment, and constant caution in our spiritual journey. Therefore, let us learn from these biblical images, always seeking to grow in faith and love and be attentive to those small things that can hinder or help our walk with the Lord.

In the Old Testament, we encounter foxes in various contexts. One of the most graphic readings is found in the story of Samson in the book of Judges. Here, Samson uses foxes as methods of destruction, tying torches to their tails and setting them loose in the Philistine's fields.

Judges 15:4–5

Then Samson went and caught three hundred foxes; and he took torches, turned the foxes tail to tail, and put a torch between each tails. When he had set the torches on fire, he let the foxes go into the standing grain of the Philistines; and burned up both the shocks and the standing grain, as well as the vineyards and olive groves.

In the New Testament, our Lord Jesus Christ Himself mentions foxes. He also says that foxes have holes, which highlights His lack of a place to live. Jesus also uses the fox as a comparison to King Herod's cunning nature. This usage demonstrates how animal imagery can vividly convey human characteristics.

In Christian tradition, foxes have often been associated with cunning and craftiness, echoing their representation in Scripture. This connection has led many spiritual writers and teachers to use the image of the fox as a comparison between temptation and sin.

Just as a fox might sneakily enter a henhouse, so too can sin creep into our lives if we are not vigilant. This interpretation calls us to a spirit of watchfulness. But we must remember that no creature in God's creation is naturally evil.

The fox's characteristics can also be seen in a more positive light. When viewed through Christ's teaching, the fox's cleverness can represent the wisdom and discernment we are called to exercise in our spiritual lives. It reminds us that navigating the world's difficulties requires innocence and wisdom.

Some Christians have seen the fox's solitary nature and habit of making dens by digging in the ground as symbols of the reflective life. Just as a fox retreats to its den, so too are we called to moments of solitude and prayer, digging deep into the "earth" of our hearts to find God's presence.

In our human relationships, these little foxes could be the small bitterness we hold on to, the minor anger we fail to address, or the little acts of selfishness we allow to persist. Over time, these can accumulate and cause major harm to the bonds of love and trust we share with others.

Chapter 16

Those Large Elephants

In the vast savannas, a herd of elephants was led by a wise and elderly matriarch. She had seen many seasons come and go, and her strength lay in her size, wisdom, and experience. She knew where the safest watering holes were, how to guide her family through droughts, and how to protect the herd from predators. One day, the younger elephants grew restless. "We are strong and fast," they said. "Why must we always follow the old one who strolls?" Ignoring the matriarch's warnings, they decided to venture off independently, confident in their youthful power. But soon, they found themselves in trouble. They came upon a dry riverbed, and the ground gave way beneath their feet. Trapped in the mud, they trumpeted in panic.

They had wandered far from safety, and none knew how to escape. Hearing their distress, the matriarch slowly but steadily approached them. Using her great strength, she began to dig them out of the mud, one by one.

When they were free, she led them back to safety along a hidden path known only to her. That night, the young elephants gathered around the matriarch, humbled. "Your wisdom is greater than our strength," they said.

"We will follow you, for you see what we cannot." True leadership is not about power or speed but wisdom and experience. As the matriarch guides her herd, we should seek and trust those who have walked the path before us. When we ponder upon the majestic creation of the elephant, we can glean profound spiritual lessons that illuminate the path of righteousness and faithfulness.

Let us dive into the depths of Scripture to unveil these hidden treasures: Despite their great strength and size, elephants exhibit remarkable gentleness and humility. In like manner, as followers of Christ, we are called to embody these virtues in our interactions with others.

Elephants are known for their intelligence and long life spans. This reminds us of the importance of seeking wisdom from the Lord and walking in His ways to live a fruitful, impactful life that glorifies Him. Elephants are social creatures that value strong family bonds and community relationships.

The biblical meaning of the elephant carries significant symbolism that is woven throughout scripture. In various passages, the majestic elephant is portrayed as a powerful creature, representing strength, wisdom, and even salvation.

Job describes behemoth as an elephant, often interpreted as having incredible might and unyielding power. This signifies the dominance and superiority associated with this magnificent animal.

Furthermore, elephants display remarkable loyalty and compassion towards one another, which parallels the love and unity found in the Christian community.

Exploring the biblical meaning of the elephant allows us

to delve deeper into God's creation and gain insights into His divine plan. Through its symbolism of strength, wisdom, memory, and loyalty, the elephant serves as a reminder of the qualities we should embody in our spiritual journey. Let us embrace these characteristics as we seek a deeper understanding of God's Word and a stronger connection with Him.[1]

Likewise, we are encouraged in Scripture to live in harmony with one another, showing love and unity in the body of Christ. Elephants sheer power and endurance symbolize the spiritual strength we can receive from God to overcome obstacles and persevere in the faith journey. Let these spiritual lessons drawn from the noble elephant inspire us to walk in a manner worthy of our calling as children of God

Elephants are known for their memory and wisdom, which helps them lead the herd through challenges, like finding water during droughts or protecting the group from danger. Explain how the matriarch's role can be a metaphor for wisdom, patience, and the value of experience. Just as the elephant guides her herd with wisdom gained from years of learning, we are also called to seek counsel from those with spiritual maturity and trust God's leadership.

In nature, the elephant's reliance on family and community reflects the importance of unity and support in our spiritual journeys. Despite their size, elephants are gentle and nurturing creatures, especially with the young and vulnerable, echoing biblical teachings of caring for one another.

To explore elephant traits, particularly in the context of

---

1. *"The Symbolic Significance of Elephants in the Bible,"*(2015–2024). Retrieved from JOHN BAPTIST CHURCH:
   https://johnbaptistchurch.org/biblical-meaning-nature/elephant

leadership, wisdom, and family, we can draw parallels to the knowledge of the elders. Elephants are known for their exceptional memory and wisdom, especially the matriarchs who guide the herd. This reflects the biblical principle of valuing wisdom and leadership from elders. Wisdom is with the aged and understanding in length of days.

Elephants have strong familial bonds. The herd, especially females, stays together, protects the young, and nurtures the weaker members. This loyalty can be compared to the biblical teachings on love, unity, and the strength of family. The unity of the elephant herd mirrors the Bible's teachings on the importance of harmony and togetherness within families and communities.

1 Timothy 5:8

> *But if anyone does not provide for his own, and especially for those of his household, he has denied the faith and is worse than an unbeliever.*

But suppose no one does not provide for his relatives, especially for his household members. In that case, he denied the faith and was worse than an unbeliever. This verse supports the idea that caring for family is a godly principle, much like how elephants protect and nurture one another. Elephants are protective, particularly the matriarch, who leads the herd, makes decisions, and ensures the safety of all members, especially the young.

Despite their size and strength, elephants are known for their gentle and empathetic nature, qualities that can be likened to the biblical principle of balancing strength with gentleness.

Like the strength and protection elephants offer their herd, God is a vital refuge for His people. Elephants are known for their incredible memory, particularly in recalling migration routes, water sources, and family members. This can be compared to the biblical importance of remembering God's faithfulness and passing down wisdom to future generations.

Romans 1:16

> *For I am not ashamed of the gospel of Christ, for it is the power of God to salvation for everyone who believes, for the Jew first and also for the Greek.*

Just as elephants remember and pass on vital survival knowledge, the Bible encourages us to remember and honor the lessons of the past. The scriptures remind us of the importance of memory in maintaining a connection with God's works, akin to elephants' memory-based leadership.

When viewed through the lens of scripture, elephant traits offer powerful metaphors for leadership, family, wisdom, and gentle strength—qualities that align with the values of a godly life.

One of the primary spiritual qualities associated with elephants in Christian thought is strength tempered by gentleness. The elephant's immense physical power, combined with its generally peaceful nature, has been seen as a model of how strength should be used in the service of peace and kindness. Christians should always show patience when helping others. There may be problems they are not comfortable talking about.

Another spiritual quality often attributed to elephants is wisdom. In many cultures, including some Christian traditions, elephants are viewed as creatures of great intelligence and memory. This association with wisdom can be linked to the Christian virtue of prudence. The need to dig deep into the Word of God is how our minds and hearts leap to new heights.

2 Timothy 1:13–14

> *Hold fast the pattern of sound words which you have heard from me, in faith and love which are in Christ Jesus. That good thing, which was committed to you, keep by the Holy Spirit who dwells in us.*

Elephants are loving and helpful animals, but we still have news that they attack humans. This is because when elephants' patience runs out on humans who kill to take their tusks or take over their habitat, elephants can also get angry. Animals have hearts, too, and they want to feel free.

Those are some lessons you can take from elephants; if you can see things from the other side, there will be many lessons you can get from around. Elephants teach many things, and the most important thing is love. Animals have feelings just like us. They want to live in peace and grow well.

Elephants have strong social structures and deep familial bonds, highlighting the importance of community, cooperation, and the value of everyone's role within a group. They remind us that we are stronger when we care for each other, which is crucial for the church's well-being. Work together, realizing that you're reaching out for the same goal.

Our understanding of compassion and respect for elders. With its dignified presence and complex social behaviors, the elephant offers meaningful spiritual lessons about wisdom, strength in gentleness, and the power of community. Observing and learning from elephants can deepen.

With their gentle strength, familial bonds, wisdom, and protective nature, elephants command a unique space in spiritual symbolism. They guide us towards nurturing our strengths, embracing wisdom, valuing our connections, and safeguarding our spiritual growth.

Matthew 11:28–30

Come to Me, all you who labor and are heavy laden, and I will give you rest. Take My yoke upon you and learn from Me, for I am gentle and lowly in heart, and you will find rest for your souls. For My yoke is easy, and My burden is light.

Overall, elephants' symbolism highlights their importance as cultural icons and their ability to represent various values and concepts. Whether it's strength and power, family and community, wisdom, and intelligence, or protection and guidance, elephants continue to inspire and captivate people worldwide.

The Christian faith should comprehend this: we must inspire the world to see Jesus through and in us. The world is in total darkness, and Christians are to brighten their light so everyone can see it. Some may not comprehend that lost souls are looking for something; we have it, and His name is Jesus.

The purpose of the church is to praise the Lord and reach out to the lost. We have a lot of work before us: helping new Christians mature in their walk, taking every opportunity to win souls, and reaching them out of the pits of hell. Time is of the essence because we do not know when Christ will return.

There are undoubtedly many evil people living in this world. We need to be aware that we don't know what we would do if left in the hands of the devil. We can all do evil when the enemy is leading us; thank God that He has our backs.

That is why we need to communicate with our Lord every day. When people stop communicating, their relationships begin to fall apart. And guess who is watching? Yep, the devil is waiting for the chance to jump on you and take over your life.

Chapter 17

The Amazing Salmon

A mighty river once flowed through valleys and forests, winding its way to the sea. In this river, the salmon were born, and in its waters, they grew strong. As the seasons passed, the salmon were drawn by an irresistible pull to leave the safety of the river and journey into the vast ocean. They spent many years there, wandering through the depths, growing larger and more powerful.

But in the fullness of time, a call would stir in their hearts, a voice as old as the waters themselves. No matter how far they had traveled, the salmon knew they must return to the river of their birth. The journey back was fraught with peril. Strong currents, hungry predators, and towering waterfalls stood in their way.

Yet, driven by an unwavering purpose, the salmon leaped and fought their way upstream, defying the odds. Some grew weary and were swept away, while others pressed on, their strength renewed by the memory of home.

Salmon are known for their incredible journey upstream to spawn. This can represent the Christian virtue of perseverance in faith, encouraging believers to stay committed to their spiritual path despite challenges. After spawning, many salmon die, which can be likened to the sacrificial love demonstrated by Christ.

This shows selflessness and the importance of giving oneself to others. The life cycle of a salmon, from egg to fry to adult, can symbolize spiritual growth and renewal. It reflects the idea of rebirth in Christ and the transformative power of faith.

Salmon often return to their place of birth in large groups, symbolizing the importance of community and the body of Christ. This can remind Christians of the importance of fellowship and support within their faith community.

Salmon face various obstacles, mirroring individuals' trials and tribulations. This can serve as a reminder to trust in God's guidance through difficult times. These lessons can enhance one's understanding of faith and resilience, drawing parallels between the natural world and spiritual teachings.

Galatians 6:9

And let us not grow weary while doing good, for in due season we shall reap if we do not lose heart.

They follow an internal instinct to guide them home, much like Christians, who are led by the Holy Spirit, who provides direction in life. Trust in God's guidance is essential even when the way is unclear or challenging.

Salmon face numerous dangers in their journey, including predators, fatigue, and rough waters, yet they press on because their goal is to give life. Similarly, Christians face trials, but their endurance leads to spiritual growth and fulfilling God's purpose. At the end of their journey, Christians are reminded to keep pressing forward, no matter the challenges, with their eyes set on glorifying God.

James 1:2–3

My brethren, count it all joy when you fall into various trials, knowing that the testing of your faith produces patience.

Even when salmon face a waterfall, they will swim and thrash vertically through the layers of water and foam to return upstream. For this reason, salmon is a created wonder that makes evolutionary theory look weak. Salmon can serve as a tangible weapon to battle our days of doubt. It provides faith that we have a God who has designed miraculous systems not just for His glory but for our benefit.

These fish begin their lives in rivers or streams. After a time, they go downstream to the ocean, where they feed on other fish and grow much larger. Then, when they have reached adulthood, they undertake an amazing journey, swimming back upstream to spawn.

Throughout history, various elements of nature have been used symbolically to convey spiritual truths and reflect the values found in religious teachings. One such element is the salmon, a remarkable fish that embodies several Christian attributes.

As we explore the salmon's life cycle and how its characteristics relate to critical Christian virtues. The salmon's life journey is a testament to perseverance. Born in freshwater streams, salmon hatchlings face numerous challenges, including predators and harsh environmental conditions, as they make their way to the ocean.

After several years of maturing in the sea, adult salmon return to their birthplace to spawn—a journey that often requires navigating back upstream against strong currents. In Christianity, perseverance is a strongly emphasized virtue.

One of the most profound aspects of the salmon's life is its self-sacrificial nature. After spawning, many species of salmon die shortly after completing this critical life cycle. This act of giving life to the next generation can reflect the ultimate sacrifice made by Jesus Christ on the cross for humanity's salvation.

This theme of sacrifice resonates deeply within the Christian faith. Jesus's selflessness, as noted in John 15:13, where He states that "there is no greater love than to lay down one's life for one's friends," serves as a model for how Christians are called to love and serve others, often putting their needs above their own.

Community and connection —salmon are not solitary creatures; they often travel in schools, representing the importance of community. Christian teachings repeatedly emphasize the significance of fellowship and connection among believers. Hebrews 10:24–25

And let us consider one another in order to stir up love and good works, not forsaking the assembling of ourselves together, as is the manner of some, but exhorting one another, and so much the more as you see the Day approaching.

It is easy to follow what everyone else is doing and encourage us to do it. It is easy to go with the flow and fit in. It is much harder to go against it and stand out. Yet, in many cases, we, as Christians, are called to do this.

Suppose something is wrong, even if everyone else is doing it, just as something right is always right, even if no one is doing it. At the end of their journey, salmon bring forth new life after the struggle against the stream. In such a way, we, having fought against the currents of the world and kept our Faith.

Hebrew 12: 1–2

Therefore we also, since we are surrounded by so great a cloud of witnesses, let us lay aside every weight, and the sin which so easily ensnares us, and let us run with endurance the race that is set before us, looking unto Jesus, the author and finisher of our faith, who for the joy that was set before Him endured the cross, despising the shame, and has sat down at the right hand of the throne of God.

Our Christian walk is like that of the salmon. We battle the evils of this dark world, often going against the crowd. Many times, we, too, come against strong opposition, but we who believe in Jesus will inherit eternal life when we die.

We, too, at times, get caught by Satan, and although Satan doesn't release us, Jesus does. He is always with us, showing us how to be free from sin. Jesus died on the cross for our sins so that we could win the victory over sin and death.

God has a plan for our lives, just as He has a plan for the salmon. Let us persevere, then, as the salmon do, year after year, and run the race marked out for us. Let us keep our eyes on Jesus until, at the end of our journey, we have reached our destination, heaven.

Matthew wrote his good news story about Jesus to help us know we can experience God being with us on our faith journey. God knows you better than you know yourself. Like the salmon, we have a rough road ahead of us.

In the Word of God, there is a place for every situation you may face. We have been assured that we will never travel this road alone. Just as the salmon swim with all their strength, they have headed to their destination as a group, so as the Christians are part of the body of Christ, they will never face anything alone.

The salmon, a creature of the waters, teaches us a profound lesson deeply rooted in biblical principles. Just as the salmon displays remarkable perseverance and determination as it swims against the current, so too should believers exhibit unwavering faith and resilience in the face of life's challenges and temptations.

James 1:12

Blessed is the man who endures temptation; for when he has been approved, he will receive the crown of life which the Lord has promised to those who love Him.

1 Corinthians 9:24–25

Do you not know that those who run in a race all run, but one receives the prize? Run in such a way that you may obtain it. And everyone who competes for the prize is temperate in all things.

Therefore, like the salmon swimming upstream, let us press on in faith, overcoming obstacles and staying true to our beliefs despite our challenges. Through our perseverance, may we glorify God and receive the crown of life reserved for those who endure till the end.

There's much more to the life of salmon than just swimming upriver. While their iconic upstream journey to spawn and die is a significant part of their life cycle, salmon experience several key stages before and after that.

Salmon hatch from eggs laid in freshwater streams. The young salmon, called fry, spend time in these streams before migrating downstream to the ocean. As they prepare to enter the sea, salmon undergo stratification, adapting from freshwater to saltwater.

Salmon grow and mature after reaching the ocean. They travel great distances, sometimes thousands of miles, to feeding grounds where they spend most of their adult lives. After a few years, salmon are instinctively drawn back to the same freshwater streams where they were born. They navigate based on cues such as magnetic fields, water temperature, and scent markers.

Once back at their birthplace, salmon lay their eggs in nests, known as reeds, in the gravel of riverbeds. After spawning, most salmon die, and their bodies contribute nutrients to the environment, benefiting other wildlife and plants. In your chapter about salmon, you might highlight how each phase of their life journey carries lessons of endurance, purpose, and contribution to the greater good.

Hebrews 10:36

For you have need of endurance, so that after you have done the will of God, you may receive the promise.

This is why we continue the journey; the destination will make it all worth it. The Word of God backs up the fact that a place awaits you. Jesus said that He was going there to prepare the place for us.

Salmon achieve what they were created to do; like other creations, God is pleased that they do the creator's will. We as Christians should follow the examples set before us and what the creator meant for humanity to fulfill.

John 7:17

If anyone wills to do His will, he shall know concerning the doctrine, whether it is from God or whether I speak on My own authority.

If we know what is in the Bible, it can direct us to the right path. There are so many avenues to take that lead to destinations that are not where the Christian wants to be. Be careful not to fall into the enemy's trap, which can lead to destruction.

Chapter 18

The Friendly Dolphin

I n the deep blue sea, a pod of dolphins lived together in perfect harmony. They would swim in unison every day, diving through the waves and singing their songs. Their melodies carried messages of peace and joy, and they watched over each other, guiding their younger members through the currents. One day, a young dolphin asked the eldest in the pod, "Why do we sing every day? The ocean is vast and silent. Does anyone even hear us?" The elder dolphin smiled. "Our songs are more than just sounds. They are reminders to one another of our unity and purpose. Even in the darkest depths, we remain connected by our song as it guides us home. Just as the Creator placed this ocean around us, He gave us the ability to sing, not for the world to hear, but for our hearts to stay in tune with each other and Him."

The young dolphin swam off, reflecting on the elder's words. As he swam, he encountered a lost and injured dolphin from another pod. Remembering his elder's wisdom, the young dolphin began to sing.

Soon, his pod heard the song and rushed to his side.

Together, they lifted the injured dolphin to the surface, helping it breathe and find strength. Through their songs, they brought healing and life. And so, the dolphins learned that their music wasn't just for themselves; it was a gift from above to guide, unite, and bring light to others in the vast, silent ocean.

Dolphins can be compared to Christians, though it may not have a direct biblical basis. However, if we were to draw symbolic parallels, we might consider qualities such as intelligence, communication, and community. Dolphins are known for their intelligence and communication skills, just as Christians are called to be wise and bear witness to the Gospel with clarity and understanding.

Dolphins also exhibit a strong sense of community and teamwork, which can be reflected in the unity and fellowship among believers in Christ.

The comparison of dolphins needing to remember to breathe to Christians needing to remember their faith and spirituality. Just as dolphins must consciously rise to the surface and breathe air, Christians are encouraged in the Scriptures to be vigilant and mindful of their beliefs and practices. The Bible repeatedly emphasizes the importance of remembering God's faithfulness, commandments, and promises.

By staying alert and aware of our spiritual life, we can continuously draw strength and inspiration from the Lord. Therefore, let us be diligent in our walk of faith, remembering the teachings of Christ and the guidance of the Holy Spirit so that we may live according to God's will and purpose. Remember the wondrous works that he has done, his miracles, and the judgments He uttered.

Dolphins often engage in joyful play. Games of tag or catch can amuse a group of dolphins for hours. Amazingly, dolphins also play with other animals, such as whales. Such sport serves no purpose other than simply enjoying the company of others.

Dolphins are an amazing part of God's creation and are fun to watch at play. However, while some are fishing, they say they run all the fish away. Could they be annoying the fishermen or protecting the fish?

I have always been fascinated by dolphins. God created these animals with extraordinary intelligence, beauty, and a playful attitude. They have many interesting characteristics. For example, dolphins each have their own "name." Every dolphin has a distinct whistle that reveals its identity, much like we have names. As you may know, dolphins make a lot of noise. However, they do not have vocal cords. Instead, they make all their sounds, including their whistle, through their blowhole.

Of all the unique characteristics of dolphins, the most intriguing is their sleeping style. Dolphins sleep with one eye open. In fact, studies show that only half of their brains sleep at any given time. So, the dolphin is always aware of its surroundings. God created the dolphin with an innate ability to be watchful. We can learn a great lesson from these creatures.

As Christians, like the dolphin and these apostles, we must always have one eye open. We must not ever fall asleep spiritually. Peter wrote that the keyword in that text is vigilant. Peter tells us what Jesus told His inner circle of apostles. We must always be aware of our surroundings to avoid the lion's attack. If we let ourselves sleep spiritually, we will be vulnerable to his attack, and he will take advantage of it. We must be aware of the influences with which we associate ourselves. We must watch what we allow in our homes through the television, computer, and music. We must be vigilant when it comes to doing the work of the Lord and not slack. As the popular saying goes, "If we give Satan an inch, he will become our ruler". May God help each of us be ever watchful over our souls.[1]

Dolphins can teach us many things, including teamwork, communication, and environmental awareness. Dolphins work together to find food, protect each other, and complete tasks. They learn to communicate with each other through clicks, whistles, touch, and gentle prodding.

Dolphins have their own language and communication methods, which they pass down through generations. They only use the resources they need and don't damage their environment. Dolphins teach younger dolphins how to use tools and perform survival skills.

God created us for fellowship, the created means for our journey to the direction in which Christ has set the way for us to follow. He knows where all the traps are and who the enemy is. He has already conquered the devil, and through Christ, we are made more than conquerors.

Romans 8:37

Yet in all these things, we are more than conquerors through Him who loved us.

Most dolphins work together to find food, care for the young, and protect each other. Humans try, most of the time, exclusively for their well-being, but working together with others is a good way to increase everyone's success and improve living conditions. Creativity is important.

Empathy is a trait most often attributed to successful indi-

---

1. Gilreath, D. (2014, July 27th). *"An Incredible Creation of God,"* Retrieved from oceansidechurchofchrist.:

　　https://www.oceansidechurchofchrist.net

viduals. Dolphins understand the plights of others by assisting members of their group in need. This makes for a cute story to tell tourists, and a dolphin's help in these trying times makes for a healthy family. What can we learn from dolphins in this regard? Empathy to our church family builds trust and healthy relationships regardless of status.

In that the dolphin must remember to breathe, it doesn't happen naturally as it does for humans. They only have fifteen minutes between breaths. If they fail to go up for air, they will die. Now, Christians should pray and study the Word of God. If we don't, we will die spiritually.

While dolphins feed, the entire group takes turns. To capture a large enough bounty of fish, the group must work in a line to ensure that food is secured. This requires coordination and trust. As dolphins create an offense to keep fish centered, each dolphin will take a turn diving through the fish huddle. In this way, each member of the group is well-fed. Sharing is an important ideal, one of many lessons about teamwork dolphins taught us.

We all need praise for our efforts. A dolphin's need is sustenance. While working as part of a team, we need a sense of belonging and appreciation. A well-fed team works better toward a task, whether hunting in the deep sea or mastering the art of teamwork in reaching out for lost souls.

Dolphins are considered one of the world's most intelligent animals, with several cognitive abilities that set them apart. Many researchers consider intelligence a combination of perception, communication, and problem-solving. If we, as humans, were to use the direction God gave, such as the dolphin, this world would be a better place. Think if we all worked together and appreciated each other.

Dolphins work together to find food, protect each other, and complete tasks. They learn to communicate with each other through clicks, whistles, touch, and gentle prodding. Dolphins have their own language and ways of communicating, which they pass down through generations. Children of God have communication skills to lift each other with the love in you coming from God. The elders in the flock know what it takes to stay ahead of the enemy; they are still living for Christ.

Dolphins can learn new fishing tricks from each other and adopt more adaptive behaviors to changing environmental conditions.

Philippians 2:3

> Let nothing be done through selfish ambition or conceit, but in lowliness of mind let each esteem others better than himself.

When we see someone in distress, our response should be to help in any way that we can. Sometimes, all it takes is your awareness or just a kind word. People appreciate that someone acknowledges them; godly love goes a long way. In the Bible, we can learn how to be better disciples of Christ.

Matthew 28:18–20

> And Jesus came and spoke to them, saying, "All authority has been given to Me in heaven and on earth. Go therefore and make disciples of all the nations, baptizing them in the name of the Father and of the Son and of the Holy Spirit, teaching them to observe all things that I have commanded you; and lo, I am with you always, even to the end of the age." Amen.

Dolphins work to help others. As disciples of Christ, we should increase our efforts to reach more lost people. Many want to see if your life for Christ is real or even worthwhile. Their answer will depend on what they can see in your life; sometimes, it's not how you talk; it's how you live.

Be a doer of the word, not just a hearer. Make a mindful effort to make your light shine brighter and help others discover their light. Be concerned about others and their needs and help meet them. Reach out and mentor new converts to grow in Christ. Worship God, praise Him, and read His Word daily.

James 1: 22–23

But be ye doers of the word, and not hearers only, deceiving your own selves. For if any be a hearer of the word and not a doer, he is like unto a man beholding his natural face in a glass.

The churches are the candlesticks, the golden candlesticks, in which these lights are placed, that the light may be diffused, The gospel is so strong a light and carries with it so much of its evidence that, like a city on a hill, it cannot be hidden, it cannot but appear to be from God to all those who do not willfully shut their eyes against it. It will give light to all in the house, to all that will draw near to it, and come where it is.

Churches should spread God's light by sharing His truth and love. The witness coming from our church and its people can point others to Christ, as anything else can't explain their attitudes and actions. People can acknowledge God and His light or turn against it. Those who choose to accept God's gift will also receive the light.

Chapter 19

The Golden Eagle

The eagle who soared alone: In a vast, rugged mountain range, a young golden eagle named Aureus lived high atop a rocky cliff. Every day, he marveled at the other birds that flew in flocks, chattering as they flew, always close to one another. Aureus often felt alone, watching them, wishing he could be part of their company.

One day, he asked an old, wise eagle, "Why do I always soar alone? Why can't I be like the other birds?" The elder eagle spread his wings and replied, "We eagles are created to soar higher than any other bird, far beyond the clouds. Our strength lies in our solitude and in the heights we reach. But though we fly alone, we are never truly alone, for the Creator watches over us."

Aureus pondered these words. One day, as he soared through a stormy sky, he was buffeted by the winds. He remembered the elder's words and flew even higher, breaking through the clouds into the peaceful sky above the storm. There, he found strength in solitude, peace in the height, and a sense of connection to the Creator's vast sky. From that day on, Aureus understood his purpose—not to fly with the crowd but to rise above, where the Creator's presence was always near.

Isaiah 40:31

But those who wait on the Lord shall renew their strength;
They shall mount up with wings like eagles. They shall run
and not be weary. They shall walk and not faint.

Like believers, the golden eagle finds strength in God's power. When we trust in the Lord, we can rise above our challenges, just as the eagle soars above the storm. Enter through the narrow gate. The eagle's solitary flight can symbolize the narrow path of faith that often requires going against the crowd. Just as the eagle flies higher than other birds, Christians are called to live differently, focused on eternal life rather than following the world's ways.

These are just a few examples to help illustrate how the golden eagle's strength, solitude, and ability to rise above difficulties can mirror the Christian journey of faith, dependence on God, and commitment to spiritual growth.

Psalm 91:1–2

He who dwells in the secret place of the Most High shall abide
under the shadow of the Almighty. I will say of the Lord, "He
is my refuge and my fortress; My God, in Him I will trust."

The golden eagle is a noble illustration of the Christian life, displaying characteristics that illustrate spiritual truths. As the eagle soars high above the earth, so should the Christians fix their gaze upon heavenly things, setting their minds on things above. The eagle possesses keen eyesight, spotting its prey from afar. Likewise, Christians should keep a vigilant watch for the enemy's schemes, staying alert and sober-minded.

1 Thessalonians 5:15–22

See that no one renders evil for evil to anyone, but always pursue what is good both for yourselves and for all. Rejoice always, pray without ceasing, in everything give thanks; for this is the will of God in Christ Jesus for you. Do not quench the Spirit. Do not despise prophecies. Test all things; hold fast what is good. Abstain from every form of evil.

Eagles undergo a molting process, where they shed old feathers and grow new ones. This can reflect the Christian concept of renewal and the hope of transformation through Christ. So, eagles face this phase specifically, as they have bald spots and lose almost all old feathers to make room for new ones. But the awkward phase is challenging, as feathers, like our hair, take time to grow.

The eagles looked patchy, ragged, and messy during this stage, but this is normal. However, it makes their lives much harder to survive and even hunt. Eagles experience flying difficulties as their wings can become unbalanced and weightless due to shedding feathers. Moreover, with unbalanced wings come low flying speeds and problematic hunting attempts.

Isaiah 41:10

Fear not, for I am with you; Be not dismayed, for I am your God. I will strengthen you, yes, I will help you, I will uphold you with My righteous right hand.

Eagles are protective parents, exceptionally guarding their young. This mirrors the Christian values of caring for and protecting the vulnerable and the importance of community and family. As impressive creatures, eagles can represent the majesty of God.

Ephesians 1:21–23

Far above all principality and power and might and dominion, and every name that is named, not only in this age but also in that which is to come. And He put all things under His feet and gave Him to be head over all things to the church, which is His body, the fullness of Him who fills all in all.

Golden eagles focus on their prey until they grab it, no matter what obstacles they face. This can teach us to have a vision and stay focused despite challenges. Golden eagles are symbols of honesty, truth, strength, courage, wisdom, power, and freedom. A golden eagle can teach us to be patient and to respect the eagle's free will and spirit.

Moses used the symbol of the eagle in his farewell address to Israel. "As an eagle stirreth up her nest, fluttering over her young, spreadeth abroad her wings, taketh them, beareth them on her wings, so the Lord alone did lead him (Israel) ..." (Deuteronomy 32:11–12). No doubt, when he was a shepherd, Moses had often seen the adult eagles "Shaking up the nest" to teach their young how to fly. The young stay in the nest from eight to ten weeks, but then it is time to grow up and discover the highways of the heavens.

No doubt, it is a challenging experience for young birds to leave the comfort and security of their nest, but this is the only way to mature. After all, eagles were created to *fly*, not to lie in soft nests, and die of overeating and under-exercising! Sometimes, the parent birds will *push* the young out of the nest! They have been known to scatter the nest and almost destroy it. Some writers claim that the parents put *thorns* into the bottom of the nest when they build it and cover the thorns with soft down. While the eaglets are small, they do not feel the thorns; as they get bigger, they press down on the thorns and finally get the point!

Moses is making this point: whenever the parents thrust the little ones out of the nest, *the parents are never far away.* They hover *over* the birds as the little ones learn to use their wings. They swoop *under* their young to catch them if they fall. And so it is with our heavenly Father: He is never far away when we are learning how to fly. He hovers near to encourage us, to catch us if we fall.

The only way to mature as a Christian is to leave the nest and start to fly. If we refuse to leave the nest, God sometimes must shake it up, put thorns, or even destroy it. Is He heartless as He does this? Of course not! He does it because He loves us and wants us to grow up and enjoy life in the heights. Sometimes, He takes away a loved one; sometimes, He permits us to lose a job or to fail in some enterprise. God does not want to see us *in the nest;* He wants to see us soaring above in the heavens. There is no growth or maturity without challenge, and there is no challenge without change. God changes things so that He might change us for the better.[1]

Golden eagles mate for life and show affection for each other for about ten months of the year. They are very adamant about caring for their family; the young eagles are taught all the skills they need to live a prosperous life.

Golden eagles are an important part of the environment because they help clean up nature by eating dead animals and keep animal populations strong by killing weaker animals. Christian families should nurture their children for several years in this world. The one thing you cannot leave out is the teaching of our Lord Jesus Christ.

---

1. Henry David Thoreau, "Walden Pond," Chapter 4 19th century.

Deuteronomy 6:7

You shall teach them diligently to your children and shall talk
of them when you sit in your house when you walk by the way
when you lie down, and when you rise up.

Sometimes, life's storms bring huge burdens upon us, and
we decide there is no way out. Just as the eagle flies above the
storm, we can reach up to the Lord, and He will lift us above
the situation.

Hebrews 4:16

Let us therefore come boldly to the throne of grace, that we may
obtain mercy and find grace to help in time of need.

When seeking renewal, it must come from the heart
because your first symptom is your lack of interest in God-
related things. We find ourselves looking at the things the world
has to offer more than seeking God's will. Then, we aren't
interested in fellowship with other Christians; they think they
are better than I am.

Ephesians 4:23–29

And be renewed in the spirit of your mind, and that you put on
the new man which was created according to God, in true
righteousness and holiness.

Instead of giving up and eventually falling completely
away, it makes more sense to stop where you are, begin praying,
and let God take over. At this point, like the eagle must renew
its feathers, we sometimes need to be renewed.

Hebrews 4:1–2

> *Therefore, since a promise remains of entering His rest, let us fear lest any of you seem to have come short of it. For indeed the gospel was preached to us as well as to them, but the word which they heard did not profit them, not being mixed with faith in those who heard it. For we who have believed do enter that rest, as He has said: "So I swore in My wrath, 'They shall not enter My rest," although the works were finished from the foundation of the world.*

The golden eagle is a noble illustration of Christians' ability to not turn from what makes them great in the eyes of the world. Christians have greatness through the Holy Spirit, which we illustrate in our everyday lives.

Galatians 5:22–23

> *But the fruit of the Spirit is love, joy, peace, longsuffering, kindness, goodness, faithfulness, gentleness, self-control. Against such, there is no law.*

Living by the fruits of the Spirit means growing in the nine attributes of a godly life that the Holy Spirit develops in people who have accepted Jesus Christ as their savior. The fruit of the Spirit is the result of walking with God. As we grow in our relationship with God and fight against sin, our love for God and others grows stronger.

The fruit of the Spirit is important because it manifests God's character within us. It is God's nature and image to express Himself through our lives. We are His children; hopefully, we want to be like DAD. This type of fruit can be seen far off and looks good to the lost and lonely people in this world.

Eagles are patient and wait for the right moment to move. As Christians, we should be patient before making decisions that will affect our lives and the lives of our families. Prayer is needed each time we approach a new adventure; we want to ensure God is with us. We know the devil can look at us with a beautiful appearance, leading us to disaster when we thought it was a good idea.

Matthew 6:33

But seek first his kingdom and his righteousness, and all these things will be given to you as well.

Chapter 20

The Sneaky Snake

All the animals lived in peace in a beautiful garden, where the trees bore fruit, and the air was filled with sweet fragrances. One day, a cunning snake slithered into the garden. Unlike other creatures, it was silent and observant, always watching from the shadows.

The snake approached a young, curious lamb that often wandered near the garden's edge. "Why do you stay in this place?" the snake hissed softly. "Beyond the garden are wonders you cannot imagine, far better than anything you've seen here." The lamb, naive and trusting, hesitated, "But the shepherd told us this garden is safe, and everything we need is provided."

The snake smiled, though its eyes were cold. "The shepherd only keeps you here because he wants to control you. Out there, you will be free. There is fruit sweeter than any in this garden if you only dare to leave." Tempted by the snake's words, the lamb ventured beyond the garden's boundary.

At first, everything seemed new and exciting. But soon, the lamb found itself lost, far from safety. The skies grew dark, and growling beasts filled the air. The snake had vanished, leaving the lamb alone. As danger closed in, the lamb cried out in despair. Just when it thought all was lost, the shepherd appeared, pulling the lamb from the jaws of the wild beasts and carrying it back to the garden.

John 10:11

I am the good shepherd. The good shepherd gives His life for the sheep.

We can rejoice because the association of the evil serpent does not have power over us. Jesus arrived and crushed the serpent's head. We hope that when Jesus returns to restore the earth, every part of creation will be included—even snakes. The prophet Isaiah depicted this harmony:

Genesis 3:14

So the LORD God said to the serpent, "Because you have done this, Cursed are you above all livestock and all wild animals! You will crawl on your belly and eat dust all the days of your life."

Just about everyone knows what a snake is. These creatures have long bodies, no legs, and their skin has a covering of scales. Most species also have highly flexible jaws or even possess extra joints to swallow prey larger than themselves!

Individual behavior varies drastically based on the species. Some spend all their lives high in the trees, foraging for food in the branches and hiding in cavities from predators. Others live on the ground or even burrow underground. Snakes are known for their unique ability to ambush their prey.

Their ability to stretch their bodies allows them to move silently and quietly through their surroundings. They can slide through tight spaces and burrow underground, making it difficult for prey to detect their presence. Snakes are often used to represent the devil because he is very sly and crafty and will mistreat you in an instant.

2 Corinthians 11:3

But I am afraid that just as the serpent's cunning deceived Eve, your minds may somehow be led astray from your sincere and pure devotion to Christ.

From Genesis to Revelation, the Bible mentions snakes in various contexts, each with subtle distinctions and interpretations. Let us dig deeper into this mysterious and tremendous theme and discover what it must teach us about our spiritual journey. The Bible clearly shows that snakes have played an integral role in the stories and teachings of Christianity.

Sometimes, the snakes represent evildoers' malicious intentions and actions, capable of causing harm and destruction. However, this symbolic imagery teaches a message of hope and redemption, affirming the power of God's authority and protection.

Understanding the snake symbolism in the Bible encourages us to reflect on our lives and how we can overcome temptation, seek healing, and embrace divine authority. Through spiritual introspection, we can confront the ongoing battle between good and evil and emerge victorious.

The Bible teaches us that we are all capable of transformation and redemption and that, through faith and perseverance, we can overcome the challenges we face in life. As we continue to explore biblical narratives and seek more profound meanings, Christians will be inspired to live lives of purpose and meaning.

Since snakes can surprise you at any moment, they

symbolize how temptations can come at you similarly. When you think everything is going well, there is a bump in the road. Not being ready for it can cause unwanted effects. If a venous snake bites by surprise, first it brings fear, then you need to do something. You rush to the hospital, and they give you what you need to recover.

Matthew 10:16.

Jesus commanded His disciples to be "wise as serpents." The word "wise" is the Greek word *pronimos*, which means *prudent, careful, cunning, discerning, thoughtful, intelligent,* or *sensible.* This word perfectly depicts the behavior and actions of snakes. They are very *careful, discerning, intelligent,* and *prudent* in acting. The Greek word for "serpent" is the word *ophis*, which is the normal Greek word that refers to *a snake.*It is a fact that Jesus told us that we need to be "wise as serpents"! The Greek means we must be as prudent, discerning, intelligent, thoughtful, and careful as snakes! There is something Jesus wanted us to learn from the behavior of snakes, so I took the time to ponder this subject. Finally, I understood exactly why Jesus used this example and how it applies to all of us regarding our families, businesses, ministries, or *any* opportunity God places before us.

As snakes evaluate a new situation, they see the opportunities in the area. They identify places of shelter. They find "hiding places" to protect themselves from attack. They observe to see where they can find the easiest prey. When all these facts are assimilated, the serpent is ready to act. But this "settling-in" period is a key time for a serpent. *And Jesus said there is wisdom in a serpent's behavior from which we need to learn!*

When God calls you or me to do something new—to move to new territory or to seize a divine opportunity—it is wisdom for us to move carefully and slowly into that new phase of our lives. A common mistake is to act too fast. Acting hastily before all the facts are gathered and assimilated can lead us to make erroneous decisions. In fact, one serious mistake can cause us to lose an opportunity altogether. It is better to lay low, stay quiet, and blend into the environment for a while, learning from the sights and the facts we observe.[1]

Ephesians 4:27–29

Nor give place to the devil. Let him who stole steal no longer, but rather let him labor, working with his hands what is good, that he may have something to give him who has need. Let no corrupt word proceed out of your mouth, but what is good for necessary edification, that it may impart grace to the hearers.

The illustration of the snake teaches us that the devil is constantly crawling around, trying to find food. His most significant advantage is the surprise attack. When the snake attacks, its victim is usually caught off guard, much like how the devil attacks one of God's children. The way to avoid such an attack is to be watchful.

Matthew 26:41

Watch and pray, lest you enter into temptation. The spirit indeed is willing, but the flesh is weak.

---

1. R. Renner, (2024, October 15th). *Rick Renner Ministries.* Retrieved from Learn To Think Like a Snake!

https://renner.org/article/learn-to-thinklike-a-snake/

Numbers 21:9

> *So Moses made a bronze serpent, and put it on a pole; and so it*
> *was, if a serpent had bitten anyone, when he looked at the*
> *bronze serpent, he lived.*

Jesus used this example to explain what He was about to go through and what it meant to the world of sinners. Jesus explained that the cross was to save those lost in sin. The lost had to look up to Jesus for salvation, which God gave His only begotten Son so that humanity could be saved from their sins by grace through faith. Like the Hebrews, if they did not look at the bronze snake on the pole, they would die, and if we do not look to Christ for salvation, we will die lost, headed to the fire of hell.

John 3:14

> *And as Moses lifted up the serpent in the wilderness, even so*
> *must the Son of Man be lifted.*

There was a time when Jesus told His disciples to move like snakes. Knowing their surroundings, He knew that His disciples would be disliked by most of the people, and so they were warned to watch.

Matthew 10:16

> *Behold, I send you out as sheep in the midst of wolves. There-*
> *fore, be wise as serpents and harmless as doves.*

Snakes have long stunned the human imagination and hold significant symbolic power across different religions. The serpent has been a vital figure in spiritual traditions throughout history. Snakes hold profound spiritual significance in many belief systems. They are often seen as symbols of transformation, shedding their skin to reveal a renewed self.

This shedding process involves personal growth, inner change, and spiritual evolution. In many cultures, the snake is seen as a symbol of healing and rebirth.

Its ability to shed its skin and emerge anew often equates with healing and starting afresh. The snake's connection to rebirth signifies the opportunity for spiritual renewal and the potential for transformation and growth after experiencing challenges or difficult times. I'm sure you have noticed that the medical field uses the snake on a pole as its symbol or trademark.

In a dense forest, a wise snake lived near a tranquil river. Though many feared the snake, it was known for its wisdom. One day, a group of animals gathered by the riverbank, struggling to cross to the other side.

The current was strong, and none dared to enter. The snake, watching from its shaded spot, slithered over. The animals recoiled in fear, but the snake spoke calmly. "Do not fear me. I can help you cross." "How can we trust you?" asked a cautious rabbit. "You are known to bite those who come too close."

The snake responded, "There is wisdom in knowing when to defend oneself and when to help. Today, I offer you my help, for we all need each other." One by one, the animals climbed on the snake's back, and with steady movements, it swam across the river. Once safely on the other side, the animals thanked the snake, realizing that while it had the power to harm, it chose to use its strength for good. The snake replied, "True wisdom lies in knowing when to strike and when to serve." Not all strength is for harm, and not all fear is deserved. Like most creations, the snake has good and bad traits. We can learn from others' good actions or from their evil actions; try to stay away from evil. Remember, the evil one has many helpers of which we are unaware.

If it feels wrong, then it probably is bad. The Bible teaches us what to look out for that could cause us to fall. That is why it is so important to include searching through the Bible in your daily life and learning the truth to live by if we remember that Jesus fought the devil with the Word of God written in the Old Testament.

Chapter 21

The Roaring Lion

In a vast, sun-drenched savannah, a pride of lions led by an old, wise lion named Aslan. His roar echoed across the plains, signaling his dominion over the land. Other animals trembled at the sound, for they knew it symbolized not only Aslan's strength but also the safety he provided for his pride.

One day, a young lion cub approached Aslan, curious about the power of his roar. "Why do you roar so loudly, grandfather?" the cub asked.

Aslan smiled and said, "The roar is not just for me, but for all who hear it. It warns my enemies, protects my pride, and unites my family. But remember, young one, the true power of a lion is not just in the roar—it is in the heart that fears nothing but its Creator."

"Will I ever roar like you?" the cub inquired.

First looked deeply into the cub's eyes and replied, "You will, but first, you must learn that true courage comes not from our strength but from trusting in the one who gave it to us. A lion without fear is not one who never faces danger, but one who knows that a power far greater than his own is guiding him."

As the cub grew, he learned that the lion's roar was more than a sign of power—it reminded him of his connection to something higher. The lion's strength and courage were reflections of his trust in the Creator who made him.

The lion in the Bible symbolizes both strength and spiritual boldness, much like Jesus is called the "Lion of Judah."

Revelation 5:5

> But one of the elders said to me, "Do not weep. Behold, the Lion of the tribe of Judah, the Root of David, has prevailed to open the scroll and to loose its seven seals."

Just as the lion roars to claim its territory and protect its pride, we are called to live boldly in faith, trusting God's power and protection. True spiritual courage acknowledges that our strength comes from God alone. The lion is a majestic and powerful creature often referenced in the Holy Scriptures as a symbol of strength and authority.

As we consider the lion, we are reminded of the strength and courage we are called to possess as believers. Just as the lion fearlessly roams its territory, we are encouraged to walk in faith and boldness, knowing that the Lord goes before us and equips us with His strength. The lion's roar is also a powerful reminder of our authority in Christ to speak truth boldly and proclaim the Word of God without fear

However, while we are called to embody the strength and courage of the lion, we are also reminded of the need for humility and dependence on the Lord. Just as the lion relies on its pride for support and protection, we are called to rely on our spiritual family and, most importantly, on the Lord for guidance and provision. Let us imagine the lion's strength, courage, and authority in our faith journey, always leaning on the Lord for our source of true power and protection.

In many religious views, lions represent physical strength, emotional courage, wisdom, and balance. They are the epitome of bravery, dominion, and the unyielding quest for freedom. The lion's assertive nature teaches us to lead our lives with authority, dominate our realms, and rule with dignity.

In the Bible, the lion symbolizes power, courage, and protection. The lion is mentioned numerous times in both the Old and New Testaments, often in the context of strength and majesty. It's seen as a creature of great power and authority, and its roar symbolizes the voice of God.

Lions stand as powerful symbols of personal strength and courage. They remind us to face our daily battles with confidence and a sense of worthiness, much like the lion spirit animal guides its followers through obstacles. These mighty lions inspire self-reflection and encourage the development of inner peace, pushing us to gather personal strength to advance despite hurdles.

Their mighty roar serves as a call to action, pushing us towards reality and courage in achieving our goals. Lions teach us to lead with strength, ensuring safety for our families and communities.

Through their actions in the wild, lions display unparalleled protection skills, taking on any challenge that threatens their pride's security.

This impressive behavior translates into spiritual meaning; lion symbolism encourages individuals to safeguard what is most precious to them. Embracing lion energy means stepping up as a leader, prepared to defend and provide for loved ones with unwavering dedication.

The lion spirit encourages self-reflection and fosters the development of unshakable self-confidence. It reminds us that personal strength is not just about physical ability but also about the resilience of the spirit. This powerful demonstration supports people in collecting their inner forces to keep moving forward with grace and determination.

Proverbs 28:1

The wicked flee though no one pursues, but the righteous are as bold as a lion.

We know the bravery of the lion, and they will take down much larger animals than they are. Through Biblical illustrations, we are to face the world without fear. We are told to be as bold as the lion, not because we are as strong and mighty as they are.

Jesus is the one that the enemy should fear, and they do. Jesus has paid the price, and no one or anything can eliminate salvation. The Lord stands stronger than the lion; He is the keeper of those who accept the gift of everlasting life. With that said, when we think that the devil has been portrayed as a roaring lion, we are being warned that the devil has started hunting for God's children.

1 Peter 5:8

Be of sober spirit; be on the alert. Your adversary, the devil, prowls around like a roaring lion, seeking someone to devour.

This symbol of predatory nature always seeks opportunities to attack or lead believers astray. The lion symbolizes strength and courage, reflecting attributes often associated with God and His presence. It signifies His power and protection and the need for believers to have faith and trust in Him.

When you think of Jesus as a lion, you think of His dual nature. Just as a lion can be fierce and gentle, Jesus embodies the power of divine judgment and the tenderness of divine love. He is the Lion who defends His people with strength and the Lamb who sacrifices Himself for salvation.

The symbolic message is that Jesus Christ stood up for us and gave us His life. They say a fearless lion would be willing to die for his group. Our Lion of Judah has sacrificed His life for our sins. God gave us salvation through His Son, a kind of love that is hard to understand. We deserve eternal death, but instead, God has given eternal life to those who accept the plan of salvation.

John 14:6

> *Jesus said to him, "I am the way, the truth, and the life. No one comes to the Father except through Me."*

In Africa, the lion is the top predator and the "king of the jungle." He's not afraid to let you know. Due to their unique vocal cords, lions have the loudest roar of all the big cats. The males are crowned with a majestic mane. As a sign of authority, they grow longer and darker with age, attracting the affection of the lioness. Without considering the religious meaning, the lion is a perfect, natural symbol of strength, courage, power, and kingship.

Let us consider the confidence a lion has. He is the king of the beasts. When hungry, he has confidence; he knows who he is. He knows the strength that he has within himself. Notice Proverbs 30:30, "A lion which is strongest among beasts, and turneth not away for any." What about us as believers? "I can do all things through Christ which strengthened me" (Philippians 4:13); that is my confidence.

Think also of the courage of the lion. A lion is not afraid of any animal. If he is hungry, he'll go after almost anything.

Do we have this courage? Think of some of the men in the Word of God, such as Daniel, Moses, Elijah, Paul, and Jesus; do we have courage as they manifested? They knew they were righteous, and so they were bold and fearless as lions. God has not given us the spirit of fear, but He has given us the spirit of love, of power, and of a sound mind (2 Timothy 1:7). Therefore, we can be fearless, just like the lion. And daring. A lion will enter an inhabited community if necessary; it doesn't worry him if he thinks he can get food that way. We, as believers, need to have some courage and daring in the Word of God.

Boldness is lacking among the average Christian today. Most do not act like lions. They seem almost scared, sometimes, to let people know they are Christians. And yet the Word says, "The righteous are bold as a lion." How is boldness manifested? Many people have the wrong idea about this.

Remember that first wonderful day when you found out what was available in and decided by your will to accept it? Did you feel like jumping? Perhaps you did inside. But it is not how high you jump, but how straight you walk, that is important after that. The night before Jesus was crucified, Peter said, "I will not deny you, even though everybody else will. No, not me, I won't deny you." This was not a display of boldness but brashness on his part. He may have said it with his lips, but what did he mean? When it came to the time of testing, he did not stand. No, that is not what is meant by boldness.

Remember Simon the sorcerer in Acts chapter 8? Simon was a bold man in some ways, but is that the sort of boldness the Word is talking about? Philip went to Samaria to help the people receive the power of God, and he performed many miracles. Verse 9 informs us that "there was a certain man called Simon, who, before time in the same city, used sorcery and bewitched the people of Samaria, giving out that he was some great one." Is that what we mean by boldness? A confident boxer once boldly proclaimed, "I'm the greatest," but someone beat him in the end. Is that boldness? "I'm a child of God; I've got all the signs of the spirit." Simon had that sort of audacity, but without knowing that truth. Simon had a certain belief in his devilish power, but was that boldness?

A lot depends on what your boldness is based. Is it on your strength or your desperation in a certain tight spot? Suddenly, your family has a sickness or a tremendous financial need. Your boldness cannot be based upon desperation. You need this boldness all the time. "The righteous are bold as a lion." Is your boldness based on a firm foundation? [1]

The Bible uses hundreds of images to describe the tremendous God Almighty. Animals and other forms of nature can help us understand specific aspects of God's character. Jesus is called the Lamb of God to illustrate His gentleness and willingness to be the sacrifice for our sins. But He is also called the Lion of the tribe of Judah to display His absolute authority and power over all creation. A lion may be king of the jungle, but the Lion of Judah is the King of kings.

---

1. P. Wade, (1997, October 15th). *"Bold As A Lion."* Retrieved from Positive Words. https://opalpete.opalstacked.com/article/wade/bold-as-lion/

Chapter 22

Water

Once, a traveler journeyed through the desert, a dry and barren land. As the sun blazed overhead, he felt his strength waning and his throat parched with thirst. In his desperation, he prayed for relief, asking God to send him water.

After a long while, he stumbled upon an oasis. The sight of the clear, cool water filled him with joy, and he knelt beside it, drinking deeply. As he refreshed, he noticed the vibrant life around the oasis: trees swayed gently, birds sang, and animals gathered to drink.

The traveler realized that the water was not just a source of life for him but for all living things. He understood that as water sustains physical life, so does God's Spirit nourish the soul. The traveler prayed again, this time thanking God for the water and the life it supported. He learned that, like water, God's grace flows abundantly, quenching spiritual thirst and bringing life to barren hearts.

With renewed strength, the traveler continued his journey, now aware that he was called to share this living water with others, guiding them to the oasis of faith.

God is moving in our lives every moment, often invisible but always at work. Water contains astonishing power that people tap into for hydropower energy, reminding us of God's greater power to transform our lives. Water, which has reflective qualities, also shows how the Holy Spirit counsels us with wise guidance. God does so when we reflect on our lives and ask for his help to live well.

Water symbolizes clarity and purity. It inspires us to examine and purify our lives by working with God to bring positive change. Water symbolizes God's great mercy toward us. As water cleanses our bodies from dirt, God cleanses our souls from sin. The ancient practice of baptism in water shows this. As people immerse themselves underwater, they accept God's forgiveness and let their sins disappear. As they rise from the water, they celebrate God's salvation gift through Christ, made possible by His resurrection.

Matthew 5:6

Blessed are those who hunger and thirst for righteousness, For they shall be filled.

There are places where people have approached a river in a desert and seen the sudden change from barren, leafless trees to sturdy, leafy oaks and willow forests by a river.

Psalm 119:130

The entrance of Your words gives light; It gives understanding to the simple.

Psalm 1:3

He shall be like a tree planted by the rivers of water, That brings forth its fruit in its season, Whose leaf also shall not wither; And whatever he does shall prosper.

Some of the world's most prosperous land is found in river channels—where a main river branches off into numerous channels and distributaries, each bringing water and residue to enrich the surrounding soil. To be a route is to be a vessel through which the great river's many blessings are delivered. This is what God's people are to be: vessels of the Holy Spirit, an ever-spreading deposited fan of thriving life in an adverse land.

Our fallen world is thirsty, dry, barren, and hopeless, like a desert with no water. I am urgently thirsty for Living Water. As Christians, we are not substitutes for the Living Water that only Jesus provides, but this water should mark our lives so that we become refreshing streams wherever we are. Every Christian life and community should be a patch of green in its brown surroundings. Like a river channel, we should be a promising environment that attracts the weary to its life-giving banks.

Our lives should be invitations for others to see the flowing spirit in us. We should remember the song many of us sang as children, often in summer camps near rivers. Water has always attracted many viewers as they stand and look at the vast sight of the size set before their eyes.

This is the image our lives should show others: the incredible love of God. We must take the river of love to them; they will go around if left to themselves. God uses the rivers to water the world around them. He uses us to spread His love to the world around us.

Water finds a way around obstacles. Similarly, life presents challenges we must adapt to, trusting God to guide our steps, just as water flows where needed. Water cleanses impurities, reflecting the spiritual cleansing we experience through faith and repentance. Calm water reflects its surroundings perfectly, teaching us the value of stillness and reflection in our spiritual journey. In quietness, we hear God's voice more clearly.

As water from a river flow towards the ocean, it becomes clearer after passing over rocks and sand beds. The further the river travels, the purer the water becomes. Similarly, Christians continue their journey with God through prayer, and studying God's Word increases their closeness to God's will. When you stop the flow, your spiritual life can become stagnant.

John 4:14

> But whoever drinks of the water that I shall give him will never thirst. But the water that I shall give him will become in him a fountain of water springing up into everlasting life.

John 7:38

> He who believes in Me, as the Scripture has said, out of his heart will flow rivers of living water.

Jesus promises that from the most profound being of the one who believes in Him will flow rivers of living water; you must stop and ask, "To what extent is that true of me? Since I trusted in Christ as my Savior, has it been my experience that ever-flowing, abundant rivers of living water have gushed up inside and flowed out of me?

When we look at water, or any other part of creation, in the light of Scripture, we see God's wisdom—whether manifested in His marvelous and harmonious works in creation or in the spiritual pictures of Christ and His work of salvation. In all His works—in Creation and in salvation—God is glorified.

What marvelous wisdom—revealing His glory in the highest possible way!

God's wisdom is marvelously displayed with the most common substance on Earth—water. Consider the following unique properties of water and notice how they are each necessary to support life on Earth as we know it. Especially note how harmoniously the various parts of creation are interwoven, showing the great wisdom of God.

Water expands when it freezes so that ice will float on water. This obviously benefits from permitting the pleasurable activity of ice skating. But there are far more important reasons for ice to float on water. Ice insulates lakes from the cold winter air—allowing fish and plant life to continue below. If theoretically speaking, ice was heavier than water, then when the water was sufficiently cold, ice that forms at the surface (where it is coldest) would sink to the bottom. In time, the lake would fill with ice, killing plant and animal life.

Again, God's wise design of water—creating it so that it expands when it freezes—displays His care for all His creatures, ensuring that plant and animal life may be sustained during the colder months.[1]

They are condemning because none of us, if we're honest, can say, "Yes, those words nail it! That's exactly how I describe my life since becoming a Christian!" Sincerity forces me to say, "Well, there has usually been a trickle of living water, while there have been some deficiencies where even it has dried up.

Occasionally, there has been a creek of living water. But ever-flowing, abundant rivers? It would be a stretch to describe my Christian life like that! So, Jesus's words convict me with the emptiness of my walk with Him.

---

1. David R. Whitlock, "Source of Life," David Whitlock Ministries Inc. 2021.

But Jesus's words also give me hope. If my life doesn't match His kindness, then something is lacking. This is a promise from the Son of God to all who will come to Him and drink: Out of your innermost being will flow rivers of living water.

Large rocks try to block the river, but they never succeed. Nothing would stop our growth with the Lord if we were as determined as the river. We must realize that the enemy will try to stop the Holy Spirit from flowing from our hearts. The continued flow depends on our dedication to serving the Lord. Through the Bible as a daily need to keep the flow rolling.

Acts 2:38

> *Then Peter said to them, Repent, and let every one of you be baptized in the name of Jesus Christ for the remission of sins; and you shall receive the gift of the Holy Spirit.*

The water of the earth serves as a profound example of Godly lessons, for it reflects Divine wisdom and providence. Just as water sustains life, so doth the Word of God nourish the soul and bring forth spiritual growth.

Consider how water flows in streams and rivers, ever wandering on its appointed path. Likewise, we ought to walk in the way of the Lord, following His guidance and leading in our lives. Let us not resist His divine direction but flow in harmony with His will, trusting in His perfect plan for us.

Through Christ's sacrifices, we are made pure and new, reconciled to God, and granted eternal life. Therefore, let us heed the lessons of the earth's water and be reminded of the faithfulness and grace of our Heavenly Father, who sustains, guides, and purifies us for His glory. We trust that the water will keep flowing down the rivers.

We must investigate God's ways, and we won't find them

in the pleasures of this world. They will deceive us into thinking that enjoying the world is what life is all about. Check out God's Word to find the path to eternal life. You can follow many directions, but remember, the rivers only flow to the ocean, and the Christian life only flows with the spirit of God.

Romans 8:14

For as many as are led by the Spirit of God, they are the sons of God.

In the scriptures, water is often used to symbolize purification, life, and abundance. Just as water has the power to cleanse and nourish the body, so does the presence of God purify and sustain our souls. In the book of Genesis, we witness the Spirit of God hovering over the waters during the world's creation, signifying His active role in bringing forth life and order from chaos.

The waters of the great flood served as an instrument of judgment and salvation, cleansing the earth of wickedness while preserving a remnant through the ark. Moreover, in the New Testament, Jesus spoke of water as a symbol of spiritual renewal and eternal life.

He offered the Samaritan woman living water, symbolizing the everlasting satisfaction of a relationship with God. Additionally, Jesus proclaimed Himself as the living water that quenches the spiritual thirst of all who believe in Him.

Furthermore, the imagery of water relates to the concept of baptism, a sacred act symbolizing the washing away of sin and the new life found in Christ. As water physically cleanses and regenerates the body, so does God's grace spiritually renew and transform the believer. Therefore, let us contemplate the intense significance of water as an attribute of God, reflecting on His purifying, life-giving, and abundant nature that flows freely to all who seek Him.

Water's ability to adapt and change shapes (such as ice, steam, or liquid) can symbolize transformation and renewal, reflecting spiritual journeys and the idea of rebirth in various doctrines.

Chapter 23

The Mountains

Once, in a quiet valley surrounded by towering mountains, a young shepherd lived in awe of their majesty. Every morning, he would gaze up at the peaks, amazed by their unshakable presence. One day, he asked his father, "What makes the mountains stand so firm, unmoved by the storms or winds?" His father replied, "The mountain is strong not because of what you see on the surface but because of its foundation deep within the earth. It is anchored far below, where no storm can reach." The shepherd pondered this as the seasons changed. Through rainstorms, snow, and even the fiercest winds, the mountains stood as they always had—steadfast and unmoved.

One day, the shepherd faced a trial in his own life. Doubt and fear began to cloud his heart like storm clouds around the peaks. Remembering the mountains, he prayed, "Lord, let my faith be like the foundation of these mountains, rooted in You, that I may stand firm through every trial."

In time, the shepherd learned that just as the mountain's strength came from its unseen foundation, so his strength came from trusting in the Lord, even when the storms of life raged around him. Like a mountain's hidden foundation, our strength comes from a deep-rooted faith in God. Even when the storms of life seem overwhelming, we remain steady if our trust is firmly anchored in Him.

Reflecting the attributes of God throughout the Bible, mountains often symbolize God's greatness, majesty, and eternal nature. They stand tall and firm, unyielding to time and the elements, much like God's character. Let's explore how the grandeur and steadfastness of mountains illustrate key attributes of God.

Isaiah 2:2–4

The mountain of the Lord's house will be established on the top of the mountains, and all nations will flow to it.

God's strength and stability—mountains are often seen as the epitome of strength. Their immovable presence reminds us of God's unwavering power. Just as the mountains stand firm in the face of storms, winds, and erosion, God is our immovable rock. In times of trial, when everything around us feels uncertain, we can trust in God's strength and stability.

Like mountains that have stood for ages, God's strength is timeless and unchanging. No force in nature can move or diminish the mountains; similarly, nothing in the universe can shake God's power. God's majesty mountains are often considered symbols of majesty because of their towering height and breathtaking beauty. They evoke awe and reverence, much like God's glory.

When we stand in the presence of mountains, we are reminded of how small we are in comparison and yet how mighty and magnificent God is. His greatness is far above the heavens, as the highest peaks point us to the heavens above.

God's eternality—mountains are often described as ancient, standing for numerous years, seemingly untouched by time. Likewise, God is eternal, existing from before the beginning of time and continuing for all eternity.

Psalm 121:1–2

I lift up my eyes to the mountains—where does my help come from? My help comes from the Lord, the Maker of heaven and earth.

Psalm 90:2

Before the mountains were brought forth, or ever You had formed the earth and the world, even from everlasting to everlasting, you are God.

Mountains endure through all seasons, symbolizing God's presence in every phase of our lives. His eternal nature means He is always with us—He was there before us, He is with us now, and He will continue to be with us for all time.

God is a refuge—just as mountains provide shelter and protection from storms, God is a refuge for His people. In the ancient world, people would flee to the mountains for safety from enemies or natural disasters. The height and remoteness of the mountains made them a place of security. In the same way, God is our protector, offering us safety and peace in times of danger.

God is a fortress and refuge for us, like a mountain shielding us from the world's dangers. We find safety and peace in His presence, knowing He will not be moved.

God's unfathomable depth—mountains also remind us of the mystery and depth of God's wisdom and knowledge.

Isaiah 40:9

> *Go on up to a high mountain, O Zion, herald of good news; lift up your voice with strength, O Jerusalem, herald of good news; lift it up, fear not; say to the cities of Judah, "Behold your God!"*

Beneath the surface of a mountain lies a complex foundation of rock, minerals, and history, much of which remains hidden from view. In the same way, God's ways and thoughts are far beyond human comprehension.

God's wisdom is deep and rich, like a mountain whose roots go deep into the earth, and we can only glimpse a fraction of it. His plans for us often unfold in ways we cannot see or understand, but they are always grounded in His perfect wisdom.

Mountains point to God—mountains remind us of God's strength, majesty, eternality, refuge, and depth. Gazing at these towering landscapes invites us to reflect on God's character and draw closer to Him. Just as mountains are unmovable and awe-inspiring, so is God's presence in our lives—strong, majestic, and eternal. We can trust His mighty strength and unchanging nature as we seek refuge in Him.

God reveals Himself to Abraham on a mountain, as Abraham demonstrates his willingness to sacrifice his one and only son, Isaac, pointing to the sacrifice God would one day make of his own Son.

God reveals His redemptive plans to Moses on Mount Horeb, pointing to a time when He'd save His people once and for all from the slavery of sin. God reveals Himself to the Israelites on Mount Sinai and gives Moses the Ten

Commandments, pointing to how He'd one day dwell with His covenant people in spirit and truth.

Throughout the New Testament, Jesus is associated with mountains. He begins his ministry by defeating Satan on a mountain and feeding his disciples the Word of God on a mountain.

He rests and communes with the Father on mountains. He's transfigured on a mountain, crucified on a mountain, proclaims the Great Commission on a mountain, and ascends into heaven from a mountain.[1]

The mountains are strong and powerful. Their sheer size and the force of nature displayed in their creation remind us of the limitless might of our Creator. Furthermore, contemplate the wisdom of God illustrated in the intricate design of the mountains. Each peak, valley, and ridge are crafted precisely, revealing the depth of divine intelligence beyond human comprehension.

Psalm 125:1

Those who trust in the Lord are like Mount Zion, which cannot be moved but abides forever.

Furthermore, reflect on God's omnipresence. Just as the mountains can be seen from far and wide, they remind us that our God is present everywhere, overseeing all creation with His watchful eye.

Lastly, consider the beauty of holiness reflected in the splendor of the mountains. Their majestic beauty points to the perfect beauty and holiness of our God, who is the source of all

---

1. Moses Y. Lee, "Don't Miss the Mountains," God The Gospel Coalition, INC 2024. thegosplecoalition.org.

that is good and lovely—the majestic mountains, those towering peaks that stretch towards the heavens.

In their greatness, we can find reflections of the attributes of our Almighty God. Consider the immutability of God. The mountains stand firm and unmoved, enduring through time and change. Our God is unchanging and steadfast in His character and promises.

Their sheer size and the force of nature displayed in their creation remind us of the limitless might of our Creator. Contemplate the wisdom of God illustrated in the intricate design of the mountains. Each peak, valley, and ridge is crafted with precision, revealing the depth of divine intelligence beyond human comprehension.

Psalm 46:1–3

> *God is our refuge and strength, a very present help in trouble. Therefore, we will not fear though the earth gives way, though the mountains be moved into the heart of the sea, though its waters roar and foam, though the mountains tremble at its swelling.*

Reflect on the omnipresence of God. Just as the mountains can be seen from far and wide, reminding us that our God is present everywhere, overseeing all creation with His watchful eye. Consider the beauty of holiness reflected in the splendor of the mountains.

Mountains serve as profound symbols for understanding the attributes of God in various theological reflections. They illustrate the splendor and majesty of God's creation while embodying spiritual significance. The symbolism of mountains in theological context—mountains are often viewed as a metaphorical connection to the divine, representing a higher realm and a closer proximity to God.

This is articulated through the idea that mountains are "closer to God," as they symbolize places where encounters with the divine can occur. The Bible presents mountains as significant meeting points between heaven and earth, where God reveals Himself to humanity.

God's revelation on mountains throughout Scripture—God is depicted as revealing Himself on mountaintops. For instance, the mountains of Sinai and Zion hold particular significance in the Old Testament as locations where God interacted with His people. This divine communication emphasizes God's desire for relationship and understanding with His creation.

Attributes reflected in mountains—the majestic and sometimes frightening nature of mountains reflects God's awe-inspiring attributes. Mountains are places of refuge, signifying God's protective nature and strength.

The representation of mountains in Scripture and spiritual life suggests that moments of divine encounter often occur during high points or profound experiences in one's faith journey.

This relationship between mountains and spiritual elevation illustrates the deeper understanding that believers can gain regarding God's character and presence in their lives. Overall, mountains in theological reflection embody an invitation to explore and recognize God's multifaceted attributes, offering believers a means to understand His majesty, power, and relational desire.

Mountains can teach several profound lessons about God. Here are a few reflections. God's strength and stability—mountains often symbolize strength and longevity. They remind us of God's unchanging nature, strength, and eternal presence. Just as mountains stand firm through storms and time, God is a steadfast refuge for His people.

Climbing a mountain requires perseverance, patience, and

strength, which can be seen as symbolic of spiritual growth. As one ascends a mountain, faith can grow deeper and stronger through life's challenges. In your book, mountains could represent the spiritual journey of moving closer to God's greatness and the strength we find in Him through life's trials.

Chapter 24

The Love of God

Once, a wise old man named Eli lived in a small village surrounded by thick forests and rolling hills. He was known far and wide for his stories, which often carried deep meanings. One day, as the sun set, a group of villagers gathered around him, eager to hear his latest tale.

Eli began. Once, a large river flowed through a valley, giving life to all who crossed it. However, the river was treacherous. Some swam across with ease, while others struggled and even perished.

One day, a traveler approached the riverbank, frightened by its turbulent waters. He desperately wanted to reach the other side, where a beautiful garden promised peace and happiness. As he stood pondering, an old fisherman appeared.

Seeing the traveler's hesitation, the fisherman offered his help. "I can take you across," he said, pointing to his sturdy boat. "But you must trust me and follow my instructions closely." The traveler, uncertain yet hopeful, agreed.

The fisherman instructed him to sit still, hold on tightly, and not panic, no matter how rough the waters became. The river roared as they began to cross, and waves crashed against the boat. Fear welled up in the traveler, and in a moment of panic, he stood up, losing his balance.

Just as he was about to fall in, the fisherman reached out, pulling him back to safety. Finally, they reached the other side. The traveler stumbled out, overwhelmed by relief and gratitude. "Thank you!" he exclaimed. "You saved my life!" The fisherman smiled and replied, "It was not just my strength that saved you. It was your willingness to trust and surrender to my guidance. Remember, salvation often requires both faith and adherence to wise counsel." Eli concluded, "And so, dear villagers, just like the traveler, we too may face treacherous rivers. We may find salvation in trusting greater wisdom, remaining calm during the storms, and allowing ourselves to be guided." The villagers nodded, understanding that the tale was not just about a river but about the journey of life—where trust, guidance, and gently accepting help can lead to salvation.

Luke 15:4–7

What man of you, having a hundred sheep, if he loses one of them, does not leave the ninety-nine in the wilderness, and go after the one which is lost until he finds it? And when he has found it, he lays it on his shoulders, rejoicing. And when he comes home, he calls together his friends and neighbors, saying to them, "Rejoice with me, for I have found my sheep which was lost!" I say to you that likewise there will be more joy in heaven over one sinner who repents than over ninety-nine just persons who need no repentance.

Salvation is one of the focal points of Christian theology, representing the deliverance from sin and its consequences through faith in Jesus Christ. This belief forms the foundation of Christian faith and practice, shaping how individuals understand their relationship with God, their purpose in life, and their eternal destiny.

The meaning of salvation in Christian terms, salvation is saving a soul from sin and its eternal consequences, which are separation from God. According to the Bible, sin is an action that all humans commit, alienating them from God's holiness. Salvation offers a path to reconciliation with God, achieved through His grace. The New Testament teaches that salvation is a gift from God.

Ephesians 2:8–9

> *For by grace, you have been saved through faith, and that not of yourselves; it is the gift of God, not of works, lest anyone should boast.*

This emphasizes that salvation is not something people can earn through good deeds or moral living; it is purely a gift received by faith. The role of Jesus Christ central to the Christian understanding of salvation is Jesus Christ's life, death, and resurrection.

Christians believe that Jesus, the Son of God, came into the world to offer Himself as a perfect sacrifice for humanity's sins. His crucifixion is viewed as the ultimate act of love and redemption, satisfying the justice of God and offering forgiveness to all who accept Him.

John 3:16

> *For God so loved the world that He gave His only begotten Son, that whoever believes in Him should not perish but have everlasting life.*

The belief is that Jesus's sacrifice can restore humanity to a right relationship with God. The process of salvation involves several key steps: The Holy Spirit works in the hearts of individuals to make them aware of their sin and their need for God's mercy. This moment of realization is often described as a conviction or spiritual awakening.

Once people know their sin, they are called to repent, meaning to turn away from sin and seek God's forgiveness. Repentance involves a sincere commitment to change one's ways and live according to God's will, followed by being baptized in water to accept the washing away your sins.

Acts 2:37-38

> *Now when they heard this, they were cut to the heart, and said to Peter and the rest of the apostles, "Men and brethren, what shall we do?" Then Peter said to them, "Repent, and let every one of you be baptized in the name of Jesus Christ for the remission of sins; and you shall receive the gift of the Holy Spirit."*

After being justified, the believer enters a lifelong process called sanctification, where they grow in spiritual maturity and holiness. Through the guidance of the Holy Spirit, they are gradually transformed to become more like Christ.

The final step in salvation, glorification, occurs after death or at Christ's return when believers are fully transformed and free from sin forever. They will live in the eternal presence of God in heaven. Salvation as past, present, and future can be understood as a past, present, and future reality. Christians believe they have been saved.

When people trust in Christ, they are saved from the penalty of sin. Throughout life, believers are continually being saved from the power of sin as they are conformed to the image of Christ.

Philippians 2:12–13

> *Therefore, my beloved, as you have always obeyed, not as in my presence only, but now much more in my absence, work out your own salvation with fear and trembling; for it is God who works in you both to will and to do for His good pleasure.*

When a person is truly saved, their life will reflect the love and righteousness of Christ through acts of kindness, service, and obedience to God's commands. Christianity offers hope and reconciliation to humanity through Jesus Christ. It is a journey that begins with faith and repentance and continues with growth in Christlikeness, ultimately leading to eternal life with God.

If we step back, stop, and look around this magnificent world, we cannot help but wonder where it all came from. Nature tells us that an Almighty God created every human being. Humanity was initially created to worship God, but we have failed. Our sinful lives have separated us from His presence because He is Holy. God cannot be near sin.

His love for us is so strong that He provided a sacrifice by sending His only Begotten Son to pay the price. Jesus Christ is His name. Without hesitation, He lived a perfect life, then gave it to cover our sins. Nailed to the cross, through pain and suffering, Jesus gave up the ghost. By accepting this gift, we can one day live in this world and reappear in heaven.

> For the individual, salvation means being rescued by God from the consequences of our wrongdoing. God created humanity to have a close relationship with Him. And He created a perfect world for us to live in. But our relationship with God was wrecked when humanity opted to defy God. That defiance was catastrophic, bringing sin and death into

the world. The word "sin" means wrong actions and wrong thinking. It is as if our sin leaves us permanently stained. God is pure and holy. He cannot tolerate sin, but He wants our relationship with Him to be restored, so something must be done about the sin.[1]

Luke 15:11–32

Then He said: "A certain man had two sons. And the younger of them said to his father, 'Father, give me the portion of goods that falls to me.' So he divided to them his livelihood. And not many days after, the younger son gathered all together, journeyed to a far country, and there wasted his possessions with prodigal living. But when he had spent all, there arose a severe famine in that land, and he began to be in want. Then he went and joined himself to a citizen of that country, and he sent him into his fields to feed swine. And he would gladly have filled his stomach with the pods that the swine ate, and no one gave him anything. But when he came to himself, he said, 'How many of my father's hired servants have bread enough and to spare, and I perish with hunger! I will arise and go to my father and will say to him, "Father, I have sinned against heaven and before you, and I am no longer worthy to be called your son. Make me like one of your hired servants."'

And he arose and came to his father. But when he was still a great way off, his father saw him and had compassion and ran and fell on his neck and kissed him. And the son said to him, 'Father, I have sinned against heaven and in your sight and am no longer worthy to be called your son.'

---

1. C. E. Agency, (2024, October 16th). *"What Is Salvation?"* Retrieved from Salvation means being rescued by God from the consequences of our wrongdoing.: https://www.christianity.org.uk/article/what-is-salvation

But the father said to his servants, 'Bring out the best robe and put it on him, and put a ring on his hand and sandals on his feet. And bring the fatted calf here and kill it and let us eat and be merry; for this my son was dead and is alive again; he was lost and is found.' And they began to be merry. Now his older son was in the field. And as he came and drew near to the house, he heard music and dancing. So, he called one of the servants and asked what these things meant. And he said to him, 'Your brother has come, and because he has received him safe and sound, your father has killed the fatted calf.'

But he was angry and would not go in. Therefore, his father came out and pleaded with him. So, he answered and said to his father, 'Lo, these many years I have been serving you; I never transgressed your commandment at any time; and yet you never gave me a young goat, that I might make merry with my friends. But as soon as this son of yours came, who has devoured your livelihood with harlots, you killed the fatted calf for him.'

And he said to him, 'Son, you are always with me, and all that I have is yours. It was right that we should make merry and be glad, for your brother was dead and is alive again and was lost and is found.'

Jesus shared this parable with the Pharisees, who were very religious and far from God. Sometimes, we get caught up in a lifestyle that has taken us away from God's presence. Many have allowed the influence of the world to take over our lives. They talk about God. Their actions speak louder; you would not be able to tell that they even knew God.

This is called backsliding, turning from our Lord to serve the thrilling sinful life; after many trials, some come to their senses. At that moment, there was a need to reach out to Jesus

Christ, our Lord and Savior, and ask for forgiveness. Some will wait till it is too late and will die in their sins.

If you find yourself without Christ, please take a moment to think about eternity and where you would be right now if you should die. We know that everyone will die, but not everyone will end up in heaven. This life is temporary; eternity is forever; our destination is according to our choice.

Chapter 25

Conclusion

Through each chapter, we have witnessed how every part of creation reflects God's wisdom, faithfulness, and care for all living things. We have explored these wonders, but we must also ask ourselves: are we living in harmony with the One who created them? Just as nature responds to God's design, let us align our lives with His will and seek His guidance during every season. The Psalmist reminds us no matter where we are on our journey we can take comfort in knowing that the same God who nurtures the oak tree, guides the eagle, and sustains the salmon is watching over us. May we always be reminded of His faithful presence in our lives as we look at His creation?

In conclusion, nature's complex beauty and profound complexity stand as a testament to the existence of a divine creator. Throughout this book, we have explored various elements of the natural world—its ecosystems, the precision of natural laws, and the awe-inspiring sensations that evoke a sense of wonder.

Each chapter has illustrated how these elements reflect God's handiwork and offer valuable lessons about love, resilience, and interconnectedness. Nature is a mirror, reflecting divine qualities and inviting us into a deeper relationship with the Creator. By observing the harmony found in nature, we can gain insight into God's character and intentions for humanity.

The cycles of life, the seasons, and even the challenges faced within environments remind us of the spiritual truths that govern our existence. As we move forward, let us carry the wisdom collected from the natural world. We are encouraged to embrace a stewardship mindset towards creation, recognizing that we honor the God who designed it to support nature.

May our experiences in nature inspire us to seek a greater understanding of the divine and cultivate a heart of gratitude for the intricate tapestry of life. In an age where distractions abound, returning to nature can redirect our focus, offering clarity, peace, and a renewed sense of purpose. Let us remain open to the lesson nature presents, allowing it to deepen our faith and profoundly enrich our lives.

Romans 1:18–20

> For the wrath of God is revealed from heaven against all ungodliness and unrighteousness of men, who suppress the truth in unrighteousness, because what may be known of God is manifest in them, for God has shown it to them. For since the creation of the world, His invisible attributes are clearly seen, being understood by the things that are made, even His eternal power and Godhead, so that they are without excuse.

Romans 1:18–20 sheds light upon the manifestation of God's wrath against unrighteousness and the revelation of His eternal power and divine nature through His creation. The passage declares that the wickedness and suppression of the truth by mankind have left them without excuse, for God's invisible attributes, namely His eternal power and divine nature, are perceived in the things He has made.

All humanity is without excuse in its knowledge of God's existence and divine nature, as they are openly displayed in His creation. So, nature is a profound testament to God's existence, revealing aspects of His character and inviting humanity to acknowledge His presence. Nature communicates that God exists and possesses qualities worthy of worship.

It conveys a basic moral order, reflecting the divine intentions behind creation. This sense of awareness is echoed in various scriptures, illustrating that the natural world can lead individuals to recognize the Creator's attributes.

Revelation of God's attributes through nature, humanity can discern God's glory, power, creativity, and wisdom. The heavens and the earth speak of His craftsmanship, as highlighted in biblical passages that emphasize the declaration of God's qualities through creation. This suggests that nature is a constant reminder of a divine presence, fostering a reverence for the Creator.

Nature effectively reveals certain truths about God, not suggesting the complete picture of His character or the difficulties of sin and redemption. It is noted that natural law does not inform humanity about the deeper issues, such as sin or the means of salvation, which require divine revelation through scripture.

Therefore, while nature provides critical insights into God's existence, it is ultimately through other forms of revelation that more profound truths are understood. Nature can be experienced in various forms—like vast landscapes or complex environments—which humble individuals and provoke a sense of awe.

This realistic aspect encourages a personal connection with

God, making individuals mindful of His presence and urging them to seek a deeper understanding of His nature. Nature teaches humanity about God both through its splendid beauty and by instilling in us a perception of a moral order that reflects God's character. However, it also reveals its limitations in conveying the whole truth of divine revelation.

Nature, with its intricate design and awe-inspiring beauty, is a powerful testimony to God's existence. When one gazes upon the vast region of the heavens, the difficult details of a blooming flower, or the recurring crashing of ocean waves, it is difficult not to perceive the handiwork of a divine Creator.

Walking out the door daily, we step into a world God constructed to deepen our understanding of him. In the Bible, the Lord is faithful to His people. Then, we step outside to see this faithfulness in the rising sun. We feel it in the rain that beads on our arm as it completes the cycle it's been performing for generations.

The scriptures describe God's design for community, and we see this communal design in the delicate, interdependent ecosystems beneath our feet.

God's Word tells us that this present time is passing away, and we confirm this as we gaze at a night sky that makes us feel tiny. The words of Ecclesiastes sink deep into our hearts as we watch leaves bud in spring and, mere months later, are tossed into the compost pile. Nature demonstrates what "life is a vapor," the preacher's refrain in Ecclesiastes, really means.

We labor in the sun's heat as we pull weeds that wrap themselves around our crops, and we witness firsthand what the Bible means when it says that sin entangles us. Fields decimated by drought show us what thirsting for righteousness looks like, and it impresses upon us how greatly we ourselves need living water.

Whether we learn from a seed that grows to produce a handful of tomatoes or find God's kindness in the shade of a maple tree, God teaches us through his creation. After all, if he is before all things and in him, all things hold together, how would creation *not* proclaim his truths?

Whether through abundance or lack, creation constantly speaks of God's power, majesty, glory, provision, and faithfulness so that his creations may glory in him more.[1]

As we journeyed through the pages of this book, we explored the profound connections between the Creator and creation. Nature's majestic landscapes, complex ecosystems, and rhythmic cycles are a testament to the divine presence surrounding us.

Every mountain peak, flowing river, and rustling leaf carries messages of hope, love, and transcendence. In our fast-paced lives, it is easy to overlook the spiritual truths woven into the fabric of the natural world. Yet, when we take the time to pause, reflect, and occupy ourselves in the beauty of our surroundings, we open our hearts to the divine whispers that echo through the rustling trees and the gentle breeze.

This discovery reminds us that we can sustain our relationship with God in every outdoor moment. Nature invites us to recognize the divine in sacred texts and the everyday wonders that grace our lives. As you close this book, I encourage you to carry the lessons learned into your encounters with nature.

May you find comfort in the calmness of a quiet sunrise,

---

1. B. Lambert, (2024, July 20th). *GCD*. Retrieved from How Nature Teaches Us About God: https://gcdiscipleship.com/article-feed/how-natureteaches-us-about-god

strength in the resilience of a solitary flower, and joy in the vibrant tapestry of life that unfolds around you. In our quest for understanding and connection, let us cultivate a sense of wonder, gratitude, and reverence for the world God has created. We do not just find beauty in nature—we see God. Feel free to modify any part to fit your tone and message better!

Nature reveals various attributes of its Creator as a demonstration of creation. However, a unifying attribute common to all facets of nature is its ability to reveal God's existence and character. This attribute resonates through numerous expressions of creation, allowing individuals to witness divine qualities.

The Scripture indicates that God's invisible attributes, such as His eternal power and divine nature, are evident through what has been created, making humanity without excuse regarding their acknowledgment of Him.

The universe is a testimony to God's glory, with the heavens declaring His existence incessantly. The constant non-verbal communication nature transcends language hurdles, ensuring that all people can comprehend this divine message.

The singular attribute of all creation is its role as a reflection of God's character. This capacity to reveal God's existence and qualities through diverse forms—from the vast universe to tiny details in nature, underscores its profound significance.

www.ingramcontent.com/pod-product-compliance
Lightning Source LLC
Chambersburg PA
CBHW071722120626
46550CB00001B/343